Now....you're cooking!
Comfort Food Classics

by
Joan Donogh

Copyright © 2003 by Joan Donogh

All rights reserved. No part of this publication may be reproduced, stored in a retrieval system, or transmitted in whole or in part, in any form or by any means, electronic, mechanical, photocopying, recording or otherwise, without permission in writing from the publisher.

Second Edition 2008
Published previously in spiral bound version

Published in Canada by:
In Formation Design
Wasaga Beach, Ontario
cooking@in-formation-design.com

Book design Joan Donogh
Front cover photo iStockphoto © Lynn Seeden
Back cover photos Joan Donogh

Library and Archives Canada Cataloguing in Publication

Donogh, Joan, 1957-
    Now-- you're cooking! : comfort food classics / by Joan Donogh.

Includes index.
ISBN 978-0-9734050-2-6

   1. Cookery. I. Title.

TX714.D65 2008   641.5   C2008-905716-3

Contents

Introduction 5

Breakfast & Brunch 7
    Muffins   8
    Coffee Cakes   16
    Breakfast Dishes   23

Appetizers 27

Main Dishes 33
    Beef   34
    Pork   48
    Poultry   53
    Seafood   61
    Pasta   63

Salads & Side Dishes 79
    Salads   80
    Vegetables   87
    Breads   91

Cakes, Pastries & Desserts 93
    Cakes   94
    Pies   108
    Cheesecakes   114
    Baked Desserts   128
    Chilled Desserts   142

Cookies, Squares & Candy 147
    Cookies   148
    Baked Squares   157
    Brownies   169
    Chilled Squares   175
    Candy   180

Index 183

*Dedicated to the memory of my parents,
Pat and Merv Donogh.
Mom was glad to make room for
me to experiment in her kitchen,
and Dad was happy to clean up the
havoc I wreaked on the kitchen
in order to sample the results.*

Introduction

Comfort foods connect us with memories of special times and special people. Typically, those times are from our childhood, when we felt carefree, safe and secure in the family nest.

I grew up in a small Canadian prairie town in the late '50s and '60s, when the greatest thing WAS sliced bread. Convenience foods were in their infancy, with frozen TV dinners (which we thought were great!) being a recent introduction. The 1950s were sometimes known as the Casserole Decade, as hearty slow cooked one-dish meals were often on the menu. Canned soup was a popular ingredient. Dinner (or supper as we called it) always ended with dessert, usually a hot pudding in the winter, maybe a piece of cake or pie. I don't think my Grandma ever baked anything other than from scratch, but Mom liked the convenience of cake mixes that were now available in the grocery store. This era also marked the height of Jell-o consumption, with recipes for new ways to use Jell-o abounding. Cookies or squares were always on hand for lunch or for an after school snack.

With the availability of more and more convenience foods, and less and less time, family dinners have evolved into meals eaten on the run. In the past couple of years, comfort foods have experienced a resurgence in popularity. In these turbulent times, people are turning to familiar foods for comfort, and it is not uncommon to find meat loaf on a fine restaurant menu. This book includes favourite comfort foods from my childhood, with some newer ones thrown in for good measure.

May you find some comfort here.

Joan Donogh
September 2003

Breakfast & Brunch

Muffins

Rhubarb Pecan Muffins

2 cups	flour
¾ cup	sugar
1½ teaspoons	baking powder
½ teaspoon	baking soda
1 teaspoon	salt
¾ cup	chopped pecans
1	egg
¼ cup	melted butter
¾ cup	orange juice
1¼ cups	finely chopped rhubarb

These are really good, the tangy orange flavoured batter goes very well with the rhubarb. Fresh or frozen rhubarb can be used.

1. In a medium bowl combine flour, sugar, baking powder, baking soda, salt and pecans.

2. In another bowl beat egg, stir in butter and orange juice. Make a well in the dry ingredients, add the egg mixture all at once and stir until just combined. Stir in the rhubarb.

3. Spoon into greased or paper lined muffin tins and bake at 375° F. for 25 to 30 minutes.

Date and Orange Muffins

1	whole orange
½ cup	milk
1	egg
½ cup	butter or margarine, softened
½ cup	chopped dates
1½ cups	flour
1 teaspoon	baking soda
1 teaspoon	baking powder
⅔ cup	sugar
1 teaspoon	salt

Excellent muffins, with a mellow orange flavour. If desired you can use orange juice instead of milk. Use a navel orange so you don't get any seeds.

1. Cut the orange into pieces and remove any seeds. Place in food processor and process until it is finely chopped. Add the milk, egg, and butter and process until blended. Add the dates and give a short whirl.

2. In a large bowl, combine flour, baking soda, baking powder, sugar and salt. Pour the orange mixture over the dry ingredients, and mix lightly, just enough to moisten.

3. Spoon into muffin tins that have been greased or lined with paper muffin cups. Bake at 400° F. for 15 to 20 minutes.

Banana Muffins

1 cup	mashed ripe bananas (about 2 large or 3 small)
½ cup	brown sugar
⅓ cup	butter or margarine, softened
1	egg
1 teaspoon	vanilla
1¼ cups	flour
½ cup	wheat germ
1 teaspoon	baking powder
1 teaspoon	baking soda
¼ cup	milk
¼ cup	white sugar
1 teaspoon	cinnamon

When the bananas get too ripe to eat, then it's time to make these muffins - you'll be glad you did!

1. In mixer bowl add banana, brown sugar and butter. Beat until smooth and light. Beat in egg and vanilla.

2. Add the flour, wheat germ, baking powder, baking soda, and milk. Mix lightly, just enough to moisten. Spoon into muffin tins that have been greased or lined with paper muffin cups.

3. Mix white sugar and cinnamon together, and sprinkle over top of muffins. Bake at 350° F. for 20 minutes.

Bessie's Bran Muffins

½ cup	butter or margarine
1 cup	sour cream
1 teaspoon	baking soda
1 cup	brown sugar
2	eggs
1 cup	natural bran
1 cup	flour
½ teaspoon	salt
1 teaspoon	baking powder

This is Auntie Bess's recipe for a really moist and delicious bran muffin. If desired you can substitute plain yogurt for the sour cream. Don't fill the muffin cups too full, as the batter will just overflow and make a mess.

1. Soften butter to room temperature. Mix sour cream and baking soda together in a medium bowl and set aside.

2. Cream butter or margarine and brown sugar together. Add eggs, one at a time, beating well after each addition.

3. Combine bran, flour, salt, and baking powder. Add dry ingredients and sour cream alternately to the creamed mixture.

4. Fill muffin tins, lined with paper muffin cups or greased, 2/3 full. Bake at 350° F. for 20 to 25 minutes, or until tops spring back when touched.

Peanut Butter Muffins

½ cup	peanut butter
3 tablespoons	butter, melted
1 teaspoon	salt
¼ cup	brown sugar
1	egg
1½ cups	milk
1 cup	all purpose flour
1 cup	whole wheat flour
1 tablespoon	baking powder

These are good on their own, or with cheese or butter and jam. If you don't have any whole wheat flour you can use 2 cups of all purpose flour.

1. In a large bowl, combine peanut butter, melted butter, salt and brown sugar. Beat in the egg, and stir in the milk.

2. Combine flours and baking powder. Add to peanut butter mixture and mix only enough to combine.

3. Spoon into muffin tins that have been greased or lined with paper muffin cups. Bake at 400° F. for 20 minutes.

Blueberry Muffins

½ cup	butter or margarine
2 cups	flour
2 teaspoons	baking powder
½ teaspoon	salt
1 cup	sugar
2	large eggs
1 teaspoon	vanilla
½ cup	milk
1½ - 2 cups	blueberries, fresh or frozen

These are excellent made with fresh blueberries. If they are not in season, frozen blueberries are fine, they will just turn the batter blue.

1. Soften butter to room temperature. In a small bowl combine flour, baking powder and salt.

2. In a medium bowl, beat butter until fluffy, beat in the sugar and eggs. Add vanilla. Stir flour mixture into the butter mixture, alternately with milk. Fold in blueberries.

3. Fill muffin tins which have been greased or lined with paper muffin cups. Bake at 375° F. for 25 to 30 minutes.

Double Chocolate Muffins

1¾ cups	flour
¾ cup	sugar
½ cup	cocoa
2 teaspoons	baking powder
¼ teaspoon	baking soda
1	egg, lightly beaten
1¼ cups	milk
½ cup	butter, melted
1 teaspoon	vanilla
1 package	(1 ⅓ cups) white chocolate chips

Unlike most muffins, these don't have any redeeming nutritional value, but they are so delicious, you won't be able to resist them anyway!

1. In a large bowl add flour, sugar, cocoa, baking powder and baking soda. Mix well.

2. In a medium bowl mix the egg, milk, butter and vanilla. Pour the milk mixture over the dry ingredients, and mix lightly, just enough to moisten. Set aside about 1/2 cup of white chocolate chips, and mix the rest into the batter.

3. Spoon into muffin tins that have been greased or lined with paper muffin cups. Sprinkle reserved white chocolate chips over the tops of the muffins. Bake at 375° F. for 20 to 25 minutes.

Spiced Apple Muffins

MUFFINS:
2 cups	flour
3½ teaspoons	baking powder
½ teaspoon	salt
½ cup	white sugar
1 teaspoon	cinnamon
1 teaspoon	nutmeg
1 cup	peeled, chopped apple
1	egg, lightly beaten
1 cup	milk
⅓ cup	melted butter

TOPPING:
2 tablespoons	brown sugar
¼ teaspoon	cinnamon
¼ teaspoon	nutmeg

A very tasty muffin that is low in fat and not too much sugar. You can use half whole wheat flour instead of all white if desired.

1. MUFFINS: In a large bowl combine flour, baking powder, salt, sugar, and spices. Stir in the apple.

2. Combine egg, milk and melted butter. Add to dry ingredients, stirring until just moistened. Spoon into muffin tins that have been greased or lined with paper muffin cups.

3. TOPPING: Combine topping ingredients and sprinkle over muffins. Bake at 400° F. for 15 to 20 minutes.

Morning Glory Muffins

2 cups	flour
1 cup	sugar
2 teaspoons	baking soda
2 teaspoons	cinnamon
½ teaspoon	salt
2 cups	grated carrot
½ cup	raisins
½ cup	chopped pecans
½ cup	shredded coconut
1	large Granny Smith apple peeled, cored and grated
3	eggs
½ cup	melted butter
2 teaspoons	vanilla

If you like carrot cake, you will like these tasty muffins. They are full of good ingredients.

1. In a large bowl, mix flour, sugar, baking soda, cinnamon and salt. Stir in carrots, raisins, pecans, coconut and apple.

2. In another bowl, beat eggs. Stir in melted butter and vanilla. Pour over the dry ingredients and stir just until moistened.

3. Spoon batter into greased or paper lined muffin tins. Bake at 350° F. for 20 to 25 minutes.

Maple Walnut Muffins

MUFFINS:
2 cups	flour
½ cup	brown sugar
2 teaspoons	baking powder
½ teaspoon	salt
⅓ cup	melted butter
1	egg
1 cup	plain yogurt
½ cup	maple syrup
½ cup	coarsely chopped walnuts

TOPPING:
3 tablespoons	flour
3 tablespoons	brown sugar
2 tablespoons	chopped walnuts
½ teaspoon	cinnamon
2 tablespoons	cold butter

Maple syrup is a Canadian delicacy, and it is put to good use in these yummy muffins.

1. MUFFINS: In a large bowl, combine flour, brown sugar, baking powder and salt.

2. In another bowl, combine melted butter, egg, yogurt and maple syrup. Pour over the dry ingredients and stir until just moistened. Stir in walnuts. Pour into greased or paper lined muffin cups.

3. TOPPING: Combine all ingredients in blender or food processor and whirl until crumbly. Sprinkle topping over muffins. Bake at 350° F. for 16 to 20 minutes.

Sugar and Spice Muffins

MUFFINS:

1¾ cups	flour
1½ teaspoons	baking powder
½ teaspoon	salt
½ teaspoon	nutmeg
⅓ cup	vegetable oil
¾ cup	sugar
1	egg
¾ cup	milk

COATING:

½ cup	butter or margarine
¾ cup	sugar
1 teaspoon	cinnamon

I used to make these at home when I was a kid and they were one of our family favourites. They taste a lot like a cake donut.

1. MUFFINS: In a small bowl combine flour, baking powder, salt and nutmeg.

2. In another bowl, combine thoroughly the oil, sugar, egg and milk. Add to the dry ingredients, and stir only to combine. Fill 12 greased large muffin tins 2/3 full of batter (do not use paper muffin cups). Bake at 350° F. for 20 to 25 minutes.

3. As soon as they are done, remove from the oven, tip the muffin tin over and knock the muffins out.

4. COATING: Melt butter or margarine in a small saucepan, or in microwave, but do not overheat. Combine sugar and cinnamon in a small bowl.

5. While they are still hot, dip the muffins in the melted butter and then roll in the sugar mixture, to coat completely. Place upright on a serving plate. Serve warm.

Coffee Cakes

Cranberry Streusel Coffee Cake

STREUSEL:

¾ cup	brown sugar
½ cup	flour
1 teaspoon	cinnamon
¼ cup	butter

CAKE:

½ cup	soft butter
1 cup	white sugar
2	eggs
1 teaspoon	vanilla
2 cups	flour
1 teaspoon	baking powder
1 teaspoon	baking soda
½ teaspoon	salt
1 cup	sour cream or plain yogurt
2 cups	cranberries

This is a great coffee cake for the Christmas season. It's good anytime really - buy fresh cranberries when they are in season and freeze them to make this later on too!

1. STREUSEL: Mix together brown sugar, flour and cinnamon. Blend in butter until crumbly. Set aside.

2. CAKE: Cream butter with sugar until light and fluffy. Beat in eggs, one at a time. Stir in vanilla.

3. Mix flour, baking powder, baking soda and salt. Add to creamed mixture, alternately with sour cream or yogurt. Fold in cranberries.

4. Spread in a greased 9 inch tube pan. Sprinkle the streusel on top. Bake at 350° F. for about 55 minutes. Cool slightly, remove from pan, and serve warm.

Coffee Coffee Cake

TOPPING:

½ cup	brown sugar
½ cup	flour
1 teaspoon	cinnamon
2 teaspoons	instant coffee powder
½ cup	butter
½ cup	finely chopped walnuts

CAKE:

¼ cup	boiling water
1 teaspoon	instant coffee powder
½ cup	butter, softened
1 cup	white sugar
2	eggs
1 teaspoon	vanilla
2 cups	flour
1 teaspoon	baking powder
1 teaspoon	baking soda
½ teaspoon	salt
¾ cup	sour cream

If you like coffee, be sure to try this excellent coffee cake recipe.

1. TOPPING: In food processor, mix together brown sugar, flour, cinnamon and instant coffee powder. Blend in butter until crumbly. Stir in nuts. Set aside.

2. CAKE: Mix boiling water and coffee powder together. Put in the refrigerator to cool while you prepare the batter. In mixer bowl, cream together butter and sugar. Beat in eggs one at a time. Stir in vanilla.

3. In a small bowl mix together the flour, baking powder, baking soda and salt. Combine sour cream with cooled coffee. Add flour mixture and sour cream mixture alternately to the creamed ingredients, mixing after each addition.

4. Spread half of the cake batter in a greased 9 inch tube cake pan. Sprinkle half of the topping over the batter. Spread the remaining batter, and top with the remaining topping. Bake at 350° F. for 55 to 60 minutes. Cool in the pan for 10 minutes, then run a knife around the sides and remove cake from pan.

Cherry Coffee Cake

¾ cup	milk
1 tablespoon	lemon juice
2¼ cups	flour
¾ cup	sugar
¾ cup	butter
½ teaspoon	baking powder
½ teaspoon	baking soda
1	egg
1 teaspoon	almond extract
1 can	(19 oz.) cherry pie filling
⅓ cup	sliced almonds

This is a great coffee cake, very attractive and it tastes great too. For variety, you can use other fruit pie fillings in place of cherry pie filling, e.g. blueberry or apple.

1. Combine milk and lemon juice. Set aside.

2. Combine flour and sugar in food processor bowl. Add butter and cut in until mixture is crumbly. Remove 1/2 cup of this mixture and set it aside to use for topping. To the remaining flour mixture add baking powder and baking soda.

3. In a small bowl beat the egg. Add the milk mixture and almond extract. Add to the dry ingredients and whirl briefly to combine.

4. Spread 2/3 of the batter over the bottom and about 1 inch up the side of a greased 9 inch springform pan. Spread the pie filling into this shell. Drop spoonfuls of the remaining batter over top of the pie filling. Combine the reserved crumb mixture and sliced almonds. Sprinkle over top of the batter. Bake at 350° F. for 50 to 60 minutes.

Coffee Cake

TOPPING:

2 tablespoons	butter, melted
¾ cup	brown sugar
1 teaspoon	cinnamon

CAKE:

1¾ cups	flour
3 teaspoons	baking powder
½ teaspoon	salt
⅔ cup	white sugar
⅓ cup	butter
1	egg
1 cup	milk
½ teaspoon	vanilla

This is an old recipe that my Mom used to make when we were kids. It's very simple and quick to prepare, with staple ingredients so you can mix it up at a moment's notice. And it is so good served warm from the oven.

1. TOPPING: Mix butter, brown sugar and cinnamon together. Set aside.

2. CAKE: In food processor, mix flour, baking powder, salt and sugar. Cut in butter until crumbly. (You can also do this by hand with a pastry blender.)

3. Whisk egg, milk and vanilla together. Add to food processor. Whirl briefly to combine.

4. Spread batter in a greased 8 inch square cake pan. Sprinkle the topping mixture over. Bake at 375° F. for 30 to 35 minutes. Serve warm.

Apple Walnut Coffee Cake

TOPPING:

¼ cup	flour
2 tablespoons	sugar
¼ teaspoon	cinnamon
2 tablespoons	chilled butter
⅓ cup	finely chopped walnuts

CAKE:

2 cups	flour
1 cup	sugar
3 teaspoons	baking powder
½ teaspoon	baking soda
1 teaspoon	salt
1½ teaspoons	cinnamon
½ teaspoon	allspice
¼ cup	butter, melted
1 cup	sour cream
2	eggs
1½ cups	apples, peeled, cored and diced

This is very good, with a nice mellow apple taste.

1. TOPPING: Mix flour, sugar and cinnamon together. Cut in butter until crumbly. (Use a pastry blender or food processor.) Stir in walnuts. Set aside.

2. CAKE: In a large bowl, mix flour, sugar, baking powder, baking soda, salt, cinnamon and allspice. In a small bowl, whisk together the melted butter, sour cream and eggs. Pour all at once into the dry mixture and beat until the batter is smooth. Stir in apple.

3. Spoon batter in a greased 9 inch tube cake pan. Sprinkle the topping mixture over. Bake at 350° F. for 45 to 55 minutes. Cool in pan for 20 minutes. Run a knife around the cake to loosen, and remove from pan.

Rhubarb Streusel Coffee Cake

FILLING:
¾ cup	sugar
3 tablespoons	cornstarch
3 cups	diced fresh rhubarb

CAKE:
¾ cup	milk
1 tablespoon	lemon juice
2¼ cups	flour
¾ cup	sugar
¾ cup	butter
½ teaspoon	baking powder
½ teaspoon	baking soda
½ cup finely	chopped walnuts
1	egg, beaten

A favourite rhubarb treat, great for breakfast or brunch on spring and summer weekends. It is also really good made with frozen rhubarb, for a taste of spring even when it isn't!

1. FILLING: In a medium saucepan combine sugar and cornstarch. Stir in rhubarb. Cook and stir over medium heat, until mixture comes to a boil and thickens. Remove from heat and cool.

2. CAKE: Combine milk and lemon juice. Set aside. Combine flour and sugar. Cut in butter until mixture is crumbly (a food processor is great for this). Remove 1/2 cup of this mixture and set it aside to use for topping.

3. To the remaining flour mixture add baking powder, baking soda, and walnuts. Combine egg with milk mixture. Add to the dry ingredients and stir or process until just moistened.

4. Spread 2/3 of the batter over the bottom and part way up the sides of a greased 9 inch springform pan. Spoon the rhubarb filling over this. Drop the remaining batter by spoonfuls over the filling. Sprinkle with reserved crumb mixture. Bake at 350° F. for 50 minutes. Serve warm.

Strawberry Rhubarb Coffee Cake

FILLING:

2 cups	fresh or frozen rhubarb, cut in 1 inch pieces
2 cups	fresh or frozen whole strawberries
½ cup	water
½ cup	sugar
¼ cup	cornstarch

CAKE:

1 cup	sugar
3 cups	flour
1 teaspoon	baking powder
½ teaspoon	baking soda
½ cup	butter
2	eggs, beaten
1 cup	buttermilk
1 teaspoon	vanilla

TOPPING:

½ cup	sugar
½ cup	flour
¼ cup	butter

A delicious coffee cake featuring the classic combination of sweet strawberries and tart rhubarb.

1. FILLING: In a saucepan, combine rhubarb, strawberries and water. Bring to a boil and reduce heat. Cover and simmer until tender (about 5 minutes). Combine sugar and cornstarch and stir into the fruit mixture. Cook and stir until thickened. Remove from heat.

2. CAKE: In food processor, blend sugar, flour, baking powder and baking soda. Add butter and blend until mixture resembles fine crumbs.

3. In a small bowl, combine eggs, buttermilk and vanilla. Add to flour mixture and blend until just moistened. Spead half of the batter in a greased 9 x 13 inch pan. Spread fruit mixture over batter. Drop remaining batter by spoonfuls over fruit.

4. TOPPING: Combine sugar and flour. Cut in butter until mixture resembles fine crumbs. Sprinkle evenly over cake. Bake at 350° F. for 45 to 50 minutes. Serve warm.

Breakfast Dishes

Baked Denver Omelet

2 tablespoons	butter
½ cup	chopped onion
½ cup	chopped green pepper
1 cup	chopped cooked ham
8	eggs
⅓ cup	milk
1 cup	grated Cheddar cheese
	Salt and pepper

A tasty breakfast dish made easy because it is baked - no watching and turning required. It doesn't have to be just for breakfast, this also makes a nice quick dinner.

1. Melt butter in a small skillet. Add onion and green pepper, cook until softened but not browned. Remove from heat, add ham. Set aside.

2. In a bowl beat eggs and milk until light and fluffy. Stir in the ham mixture and 1/2 cup of the Cheddar cheese. Season with salt and pepper.

3. Pour into a greased 9 inch square or 10 inch round baking dish. Sprinkle the remaining 1/2 cup of cheese over top. Bake at 400° F. for 20 to 25 minutes, until golden brown. Makes 4 to 6 servings.

Pancakes

1½ cups	flour
3½ teaspoons	baking powder
¾ teaspoon	salt
2 tablespoons	sugar
1	egg, beaten
1¾ cups	milk
3 tablespoons	melted butter

I learned to make pancakes in 4H club when I was a kid, and I have been making them ever since.

1. Combine flour, baking powder, salt and sugar together in a large bowl.

2. In a small bowl, combine egg, milk and butter. Add to the flour mixture and beat until smooth.

3. Drop by large spoonfuls or 1/4 cup measure onto hot griddle. Cook until the top is full of bubbles, then flip and cook the other side. Serve with butter and syrup.

Breakfast Strata

16 slices	white bread, crusts removed
	Thinly sliced ham
	Slices of Cheddar cheese (or 1 cup grated)
6	eggs
½ teaspoon	salt
¼ teaspoon	pepper
1 teaspoon	dry mustard
¼ cup	minced onion
¼ cup	finely chopped red or green pepper
1 teaspoon	Worchestershire sauce
Dash	red pepper sauce
3 cups	milk
¼ cup	butter
½ cup	crushed cereal (optional)

This recipe is sometimes called "Christmas Morning Wife Saver" as you prepare it the night before and on Christmas morning you can just pop it in the oven to bake while the presents are being opened.

1. The night before: Butter a 9 x 13 inch baking dish. Arrange 8 slices of bread in the bottom of the dish. Top each slice of bread with 1 or 2 slices of ham, and slices of Cheddar cheese. If using grated Cheddar cheese sprinkle it evenly over top. Cover with the remaining 8 slices of bread (so you have 8 sandwiches).

2. Beat eggs, add salt, pepper, mustard, onions, chopped pepper, Worchestershire sauce and red pepper sauce. Stir in milk. Pour the egg mixture over the sandwiches. Cover and refrigerate over night.

3. In the morning: Melt the butter and pour over top. Top with crushed cereal, like corn flakes, rice krispies, etc. if desired. (It makes it look pretty.) Bake, uncovered, for 1 hour at 350° F. Remove from the oven and let stand for 10 minutes before serving. Makes 6 to 8 servings.

Baked Apple French Toast

¼ cup	butter
½ cup	brown sugar
1 tablespoon	corn syrup
2	apples, peeled and thinly sliced
½ loaf	French bread, sliced
2	eggs
¾ cup	milk
½ teaspoon	vanilla

What could be better than French Toast? French Toast with apples! This is very easy too.

1. The night before: Melt butter, stir in brown sugar and syrup. Spread in the bottom of a 9 x 13 inch baking pan. Arrange apple slices over top. Place bread slices over top of apples.

2. Beat eggs until light. Add milk and vanilla. Pour evenly over bread. Cover and refrigerate overnight.

3. In the morning: Preheat oven to 350° F. Bake, uncovered, for about 40 minutes, until bread is golden brown. Serve with syrup.

Extra Recipes

Appetizers

Appetizers

Cheese Ball

2 packages	(8 oz. each) cream cheese
2 cups	shredded Cheddar cheese
1 tablespoon	chopped pimento
1 tablespoon	chopped green pepper
1 tablespoon	chopped onion
2 teaspoons	Worchestershire sauce
1 teaspoon	lemon juice
Dash	red pepper sauce
Dash	salt
	Chopped pecans

When I was a kid, we thought a cheese ball was about the fanciest appetizer around, and was a special treat reserved for Christmas. This recipe is easy to make, and tastes even better than the cheese balls you can buy.

1. Soften cream cheese to room temperature. Combine cream cheese and Cheddar cheese in food processor, and blend until smooth.

2. Add all the remaining ingredients, except pecans, and mix well. Shape into a ball or a log, and roll in pecans. Chill for several hours. Serve with crackers.

Hot Crab Dip

1 package	(8 oz.) cream cheese, softened
¼ cup	mayonnaise
1 teaspoon	lemon juice
¼ cup	finely chopped onion
1 can	crab meat
½ cup grated	Parmesan cheese

This is an easy and tasty dip that you can whip up at a moment's notice. If you have a can of crab meat in the cupboard and a package of cream cheese in the fridge, the rest of the ingredients you probably already have on hand. You can use low-fat cream cheese and mayonnaise in this recipe.

1. Blend cream cheese and mayonnaise together until smooth. Stir in remaining ingredients.

2. Spread mixture in a 9 inch pie plate. Bake at 375° F. for 18 to 20 minutes, until heated through and lightly browned. Serve immediately with crackers.

Shrimp Spread

1 package	(8 oz.) cream cheese, softened
1 tablespoon	ketchup
2 tablespoons	Miracle Whip salad dressing
¼ teaspoon	dry mustard
¼ teaspoon	garlic salt
¼ teaspoon	Worchestershire sauce
1 can	(4 oz.) salad shrimp, drained
2 tablespoons	chopped dill pickle

A tasty spread. Salad shrimp are the teeny tiny ones, which also have the benefit of being inexpensive. If using larger shrimp, chop them before adding to the cream cheese mixture. Reserve a few shrimp to decorate the top.

1. Combine cream cheese, ketchup, Miracle Whip, mustard, garlic salt and Worchestershire sauce. Blend until smooth. Stir in shrimp and dill pickle.

2. Pack into a serving dish, and refrigerate for at least 2 hours. Serve with crackers to spread it on.

Stuffed Mushrooms

24	large mushrooms, 1 ½ to 2 inch diameter
3 tablespoons	butter
¼ cup	finely chopped onion
1 teaspoon	Worchestershire sauce
¾ cup	fresh breadcrumbs
¾ cup	shredded Cheddar cheese
	Salt and pepper

A classic appetizer. For party convenience you can stuff the mushrooms early in the day, or the day before, and store them in the fridge. Then just pop them in the oven when you are ready to serve. You can make breadcrumbs by whirling fresh bread or rolls in the food processor or blender - don't use dry breadcrumbs you need the moisture of the bread.

1. Wash and dry the mushrooms. Remove the stems from the mushroom caps. Reserve the mushroom caps, and finely chop the stems.

2. Heat the butter in a skillet. Add the chopped mushroom stems and the onion. Saute until they are soft. Remove from heat, stir in Worchestershire sauce, breadcrumbs, cheese and salt and pepper.

3. Spoon the bread mixture into the mushroom caps, mounding over the top. Pour 1/3 cup of water in a shallow baking dish. Place stuffed mushroom caps in the dish. Bake at 350° F. for 20 minutes. Remove from oven, arrange on a serving tray and serve immediately.

Appetizers

Cheddar Shortbread

¾ cup	butter, softened
¼ teaspoon	dry mustard
½ teaspoon	freshly ground pepper
1½ cups	grated old Cheddar cheese
1¼ cups	flour

For a festive appetizer, use fancy cookie cutters to cut these savoury shortbreads. You can sprinkle the cookies with chopped pecans or other nuts before baking if desired.

1. Combine butter, mustard and pepper in food processor, and whirl to combine. Add cheese and whirl again to mix. Add flour and pulse just until blended.

2. Roll dough out on a lightly floured surface, to 1/4 inch thickness. Cut with desired small cookie cutter and transfer to cookie sheet. Bake at 350° F. for about 20 minutes, until lightly browned on the bottom.

Baked Cranberry Brie

¼ cup	butter, melted
4 sheets	phyllo pastry
1 round	(8 oz.) of Brie cheese
3 tablespoons	cranberry sauce

A great holiday appetizer: easy to make, and very attractive and tasty.

1. Brush the top of each sheet of phyllo pastry with melted butter. Layer them on top of each other.

2. Place the Brie in the centre of the pastry. Top with the cranberry sauce. Bring the phyllo dough up to enclose the Brie, and twist the edges together. Brush with the remaining butter. Bake at 400° F. for 20 minutes, until the crust is nicely browned. Let cool for 20 minutes, and cut into triangles to serve.

Smoked Salmon Pate

¼ pound	smoked salmon
1 can	(7 oz.) red salmon
1 package	(4 oz.) cream cheese
¼ cup	butter, softened

This is a super simple appetizer. You can make it at a moment's notice, or a day ahead of time. Any leftover pate makes a great sandwich too.

1. Combine all ingredients in food processor, and process until smooth. Pack into a serving dish.

2. Store in the fridge. Serve with crackers or small pieces of bread to spread it on. Add capers or dill to garnish if desired.

Sweet and Sour Meatballs

MEATBALLS:

1	egg, lightly beaten
½ cup	soft breadcrumbs
¼ cup	milk
⅓ cup	finely chopped onion
1 teaspoon	salt
½ teaspoon	Worcestershire sauce
1 pound	ground beef

SAUCE:

½ cup	ketchup
⅓ cup	sugar
⅓ cup	vinegar
1 tablespoon	Worcestershire sauce

Meatballs are always a popular appetizer. Serve with fancy toothpicks in order to pick them up. You can make the meatballs and brown them early in the day, and store in the fridge. Then combine with the sauce and bake just before serving.

1. MEATBALLS: Combine all ingredients in a large bowl. Mix well. Shape into 1 inch meatballs and brown in frying pan over medium heat. Drain off fat and transfer to a 2 1/2 quart baking dish.

2. SAUCE: Combine sauce ingredients. Pour over meatballs. Bake, uncovered, at 350° F. for 45 to 60 minutes, until meatballs are cooked through. Stir occasionally. Remove from the oven and transfer to a serving dish. Serve immediately.

Guacamole

2	ripe medium avocados
½ cup	Miracle Whip salad dressing
1 clove	garlic
1 tablespoon	lime juice
Dash	hot sauce

Another quick and easy dip. A must for a Mexican themed dinner.

1. Peel and seed the avocados. Place in food processor. Add remaining ingredients and whirl until smooth.

2. Spoon into a serving dish and serve immediately with tortilla chips.

Spinach Dip

1 package	(10 oz.) fresh spinach
1 cup	mayonnaise
1 cup	sour cream
1 package	dry vegetable soup mix
2	round pumpernickel bread loaves

A very impressive looking appetizer - and it's so easy! You can use light mayonnaise and plain yogurt to reduce the fat content. You can also use Miracle Whip salad dressing instead of mayonnaise, for a zippier taste.

1. Wash spinach and drain well. Cook in a pot with the water clinging to the leaves, just until tender and wilted. Drain and squeeze out any remaining water. Chop finely.

2. Combine mayonnaise, sour cream, and soup mix. Add chopped spinach and stir to combine. Refrigerate for at least 3 hours.

3. Cut the top off of one of the pumpernickel loaves. Scoop the bread out of the centre of the loaf, so you are left with a bowl. Cut the scooped out bread, and the second loaf of bread, into bite sized pieces. Just before serving, spoon dip into pumpernickel bowl, place on serving platter. Surround with bread pieces.

Nuts and Bolts

1	small box Shreddies cereal
1	small box Cheerios cereal
1 pound	mixed nuts
1 package	pretzels
1 tablespoon	Worchestershire sauce
1 teaspoon	celery salt
1 teaspoon	onion salt
1 teaspoon	garlic salt
1 cup	peanut oil or Crisco oil

My brother Stephen was well known, and very popular, for making big batches of Nuts and Bolts for the Christmas holidays. You can vary the ingredients to your taste.

1. Combine cereals, nuts, and pretzels together in a large roasting pan.

2. Mix oil and seasonings together. Pour over the cereal mixture. Bake, uncovered, at 200° F. for 2 hours, stirring every 20 minutes. Cool and pack in containers to store. Can be frozen.

Main Dishes

Beef

Oven Pot Roast

3 pound	beef roast
2 tablespoons	olive oil
1	large onion, sliced
4	medium carrots, cut in 1 inch pieces
1 can	(28 oz.) stewed tomatoes
2 cups	red wine
2 cups	beef broth
2 tablespoons	dried parsley
6 cloves	garlic, minced
2	bay leaves
2 teaspoons	dried thyme
½ teaspoon	freshly ground pepper
6	medium potatoes, peeled and cut in quarters

A great Sunday meal! It's a little fancier than the roast beef Grandma used to make every other Sunday. Vegetables cooked along with the roast like this taste so good.

1. Preheat oven to 375° F. Heat oil in a frying pan, and brown meat on all sides. Transfer meat to a large casserole dish or roaster.

2. Add all the remaining ingredients, except the potatoes, to the casserole dish. The liquid should cover the vegetables and meat. Add more broth or water if necessary.

3. Cover, and bake in preheated oven for 2 hours. Turn the beef after an hour. Add potatoes to the pan, increase the oven temperature to 400° F. and bake uncovered for about 1 hour, until meat and potatoes are tender. Turn meat every 15 minutes. Makes about 6 servings.

Steak Chili

2 tablespoons	vegetable oil
2 cups	chopped onion
4 cloves	garlic, minced
1	large red pepper, cubed
1 cup	chopped celery
1 pound	sirloin steak, cut into ½ inch cubes
2 tablespoons	chili powder
1 teaspoon	cumin
½ teaspoon	leaf oregano
1 can	(28 oz.) stewed tomatoes, with juice
1 can	(5 ½ oz.) tomato paste
2 cans	(19 oz. each) red kidney beans, drained
1 tablespoon	lemon juice
2 teaspoons	Worchestershire sauce
½ teaspoon	hot sauce
	Salt and pepper

This is a great chili, made with steak instead of ground beef. Shredded Cheddar cheese is a nice touch to garnish the bowls. You can use round steak or other less expensive cuts of beef, but simmer it longer.

1. In a large saucepan or Dutch oven, heat 1 tablespoon oil, and cook the onion and garlic over medium heat for 5 minutes. Add pepper and celery and cook another 5 minutes, until softened. Remove vegetables from the pan. Add the remaining oil, and brown the steak cubes in batches.

2. When all the steak has been browned, return the vegetables and steak cubes to the pan over low heat. Add the chili powder, cumin and oregano. Cook and stir for one minute.

3. Add the tomatoes, tomato paste, and kidney beans. Bring to a boil, then reduce heat, cover and simmer for about 45 minutes, until meat is tender.

4. Stir in lemon juice, Worchestershire sauce, hot sauce, and salt and pepper. Remove from heat. Makes about 6 servings.

Braised Garlic Short Ribs

4 pounds	beef short ribs
2 - 3 tbsp.	oil
1 can	(19 oz.) tomatoes
2 cups	beef bouillon
2	onions, sliced
4 cloves	garlic, crushed
2 tbsp.	brown sugar
1½ tbsp.	chili powder
1 teaspoon	oregano
1 teaspoon	basil
¼ teaspoon	crushed dried chilies

A good recipe for an inexpensive cut of meat. Ribs have to cook for a long time, but then they are really tender, and this sauce is delicious.

1. Heat oil in a large frying pan. Cut ribs into 2 inch pieces. Add 3 or 4 pieces at a time and cook until browned on all sides. Remove to a plate when they are done, and continue until all meat is browned.

2. In a large casserole dish mix the remaining ingredients. Break up the tomatoes if whole. Submerge the ribs in the mixture and cover. Bake at 325° F. for 2 1/2 to 3 hours, until the meat is fork tender. Turn the ribs at least once during cooking and stir occasionally. Makes 4 servings.

Swiss Steak

1½ pounds	round steak, ¾ inch thick
3 tablespoons	flour
1 teaspoon	salt
¼ teaspoon	pepper
2 tablespoons	oil
½	bay leaf
½ teaspoon	Worcestershire sauce
2 cups	hot water
1 cup	chopped onion
½ cup	chopped celery

The slow cooking makes an inexpensive cut of meat nice and tender. You can cook the meat in one piece, or cut it into serving size portions before cooking. The sauce makes a nice tasty gravy to serve with mashed potatoes.

1. With a meat pounder or edge of a saucer, pound flour, salt and pepper into both sides of steak. In a large skillet heat oil and brown the steak on both sides. Add bay leaf, Worcestershire sauce, and water. Cover and simmer for 3 hours, turning occasionally. A

2. dd onion and celery for the last 1/2 hour. Remove bay leaf and serve. Makes 4 servings.

Beef Bourguignon

3 pounds	lean beef
⅓ cup	butter
¾ pound	small mushrooms
1 cup	small pearl onions, peeled
¼ cup	flour
2 cups	beef bouillon
2 cups	red wine
1 can	(5 ½ oz.) tomato paste
4 cloves	garlic, crushed
1 teaspoon	salt
1 teaspoon	thyme
1	bay leaf
	Pepper
	Chopped parsley

A classic - and one of my favourite company dinners. Serve it with fresh bread, and of course, red wine.

1. Cut beef into bite sized cubes. In a large skillet heat half of the butter. Add the mushrooms and brown very lightly. Remove and set aside. Add the remaining butter to the pan and brown the onions. Remove and set aside.

2. Add beef cubes to the pan in batches, browning on all sides. Remove cubes as done, and continue until all beef has been browned. Remove all beef cubes and set aside.

3. To the remaining fat in the pan stir the flour, then add the bouillon, wine and tomato paste. Bring to a boil and stir until thickened. Add garlic, salt, thyme, bay leaf and freshly ground pepper.

4. Mix sauce and meat cubes together in a large casserole dish. Cover and bake at 350° F. for about 2 hours, until the meat is very tender.

5. Add the onions for the last half hour of cooking time, and the mushrooms for the last 15 minutes. Remove from oven and remove bay leaf. Sprinkle fresh parsley over top. Makes 6 to 8 servings.

Spicy Beef Goulash

2 pounds	lean beef
4 slices	bacon, chopped
2	medium onions, sliced
1 tablespoon	paprika
1 teaspoon	salt
¼ teaspoon	pepper
2 cloves	garlic, minced
½ teaspoon	caraway seeds
1	large green pepper, chopped
1 can	(19 oz.) tomatoes
2 tablespoons	flour
1 cup	sour cream

This is excellent! Serve it over egg noodles.

1. Cut beef into bite sized cubes. In a heavy saucepan brown the bacon. Add onion and cook until softened. Add the paprika and cook and stir for 30 seconds. Then add the meat cubes and all other ingredients except the flour and sour cream.

2. Cover and cook over low heat until meat is tender, about 1 1/2 hours, stirring often. Just before serving, mix the flour and sour cream together and stir into the goulash. Do not boil. Makes 4 to 6 servings.

Steak and Mushroom Casserole

2 pounds	sirloin steak
⅓ cup	flour
1 teaspoon	salt
¼ teaspoon	pepper
1 tbsp.	dry mustard
2 tbsp.	olive oil
2½ cups	sliced mushrooms
1	medium onion, sliced
2 tbsp.	red wine
3 tbsp.	brown sugar
1½ tbsp.	Worcestershire sauce
1 can	(19 oz.) tomatoes

I like this with rice but you could serve it with potatoes or egg noodles, or crusty bread would be good too.

1. Cut beef into bite sized cubes. Combine flour, salt, pepper and dry mustard. Toss beef cubes in the flour mixture to coat. Heat oil in a large frying pan, and brown beef cubes on all sides. Brown in batches and remove as done. Add more oil if necessary.

2. Place the browned beef cubes in a large casserole dish. Add the remaining ingredients. Cover and bake at 350° F. for 1 1/2 to 2 hours, until tender. Stir occasionally. Makes 6 servings.

Devilled Swiss Steak

1½ pounds	top round steak, 1 inch thick
1 tablespoon	dry mustard
½ cup	flour
	Salt and pepper
2 tablespoons	oil
1 cup	sliced onions
1	diced carrot
1 can	(14 oz.) tomatoes
2 tablespoons	Worcestershire sauce
1 tablespoon	brown sugar

This makes a yummy sweet and sour sauce. I like it served with rice, but back home we would have it with potatoes.

1. Mix dry mustard and flour together. Pound into both sides of the steak. Season with salt and pepper. Heat the oil in a frying pan and brown the meat on both sides.

2. Transfer to a small roaster or a casserole dish. Pour the remaining ingredients over top. Bake at 325° F. for 1 1/2 hours. Makes 4 servings.

Mock Duck (Stuffed Steak)

1½ pounds	round steak, about ¾ inch thick
1½ cups	soft breadcrumbs
1 teaspoon	parsley
1 teaspoon	thyme
½ teaspoon	salt
⅛ teaspoon	pepper
1	small onion, chopped
1½ tbsp.	melted butter
1 cup	boiling water
2 tbsp.	melted butter
2½ tbsp.	flour
⅓ cup	cold water

Who said you needed a chicken or a turkey to give you the excuse for stuffing? Here is a recipe for stuffed steak that my Mom used to make. I don't think it looks anything like a duck, but it is good! Nice with mashed potatoes and peas.

1. Pound the steak with a meat pounder to tenderize and flatten it. Mix the breadcrumbs, parsley, thyme, salt, pepper, onion and 1 1/2 tablespoons of melted butter together to make a stuffing.

2. Spread the stuffing mixture, like a log, down the center of the steak. Bring the sides of the steak around the stuffing, so that you have a tube (like a stuffed cannelloni).

3. Tie the steak tube so that it stays in shape. Place in a small roasting pan. Mix the boiling water and remaining butter, and pour over the "duck." Cover and bake at 325° F. for 2 1/2 hours. Remove to a platter.

4. To make gravy, pour the pan juices into a small saucepan. Make a paste with the flour and cold water and whisk into the saucepan. Heat and stir until thickened. Makes 4 to 6 servings.

Burgundy Beef Stew

2 pounds	lean stewing beef, cut in 1 inch cubes
3 tablespoons	flour
½ teaspoon	salt
¼ teaspoon	pepper
2 tablespoons	vegetable oil
3	carrots, sliced crosswise into ¼ to ½ inch pieces
2 cloves	garlic, minced
1 cup	beef stock
¾ cup	red wine
2	bay leaves
½ teaspoon	thyme
1 pound	small mushrooms
½ pound	pearl onions, peeled

This is a very tasty stew. The pearl onions make it fancier, but if you can't find any, or don't have time to peel them, you can just use a cup or so of chopped onion - add with the carrots and garlic. Garnish with parsley if you like.

1. Mix flour and salt and pepper together. Pour over the beef cubes and toss to coat beef with flour. In a large saucepan or Dutch oven, heat 1 tablespoon oil, and brown the beef cubes in batches. Brown on all sides, and add more oil if necessary. Remove beef from the pan.

2. Add the remaining oil, and carrots and garlic. Cook for about 3 minutes.

3. Return beef to the pan. Add beef stock, wine, bay leaves and thyme. Bring to a boil, reduce heat, cover and simmer for about an hour.

4. Add the pearl onions and mushrooms and simmer for another 30 minutes, or until tender. Remove from heat and discard bay leaves. Makes 6 to 8 servings.

Beef and Broccoli Stir Fry

1 pound	sirloin steak, ¾ inch thick
1 tablespoon	vegetable oil
3 cups	broccoli pieces
2 cloves	garlic, minced
1 can	(10 oz.) tomato soup
3 tablespoons	soy sauce
1 tablespoon	vinegar

Tomato soup goes Oriental in this tasty stir fry sauce. Serve over rice.

1. Slice beef into very thin strips. In a skillet or wok, heat oil. Add beef and stir fry until beef is cooked.

2. Add broccoli and garlic and cook until broccoli is tender-crisp. Add soup, soy sauce and vinegar. Heat and stir until boiling. Makes 4 servings.

Steak and Onion Stir Fry

½ pound	round steak
2	small unpeeled potatoes
2	small onions
1 clove	garlic
¼ pound	fresh mushrooms
1 cup	frozen peas
1 cup	fresh or frozen green beans
2 tablespoons	olive oil
2 tablespoons	butter
¼ teaspoon	thyme
	Salt and pepper

This is a great idea for a weekday "meal in a hurry": it's really quick to make, inexpensive, nutritious, and it's really good too.

1. Slice meat into bite size strips. Scrub potatoes and cut into 1/2 inch wedges. Slice onions and separate into rings. Mince garlic. Thickly slice mushrooms. Measure out the peas. Slice fresh beans or measure out frozen beans.

2. In a large skillet or wok heat oil and stir fry the meat for about 2 minutes. Add the butter, heat to melt it, and then add the potatoes. Stir fry until they start to brown, about 4 minutes.

3. Add the remaining ingredients and stir fry until the vegetables are heated through and the meat is done, about 4 more minutes. Makes 2 to 4 servings.

Hamburger Soup

1½ pounds	ground beef
1	large onion, chopped
2 - 4 cloves	garlic, minced
1 can	(28 oz.) stewed tomatoes
2 cups	water
3 cups	beef broth
1 can	(10 oz.) tomato soup
4	large carrots, chopped
3 stalks	celery, chopped
½ cup	barley
1	bay leaf
1 tablespoon	dried parsley
1 teaspoon	dried basil
	Pepper

This is a very thick, hearty soup. Just add some crusty bread or rolls and you have a great meal.

1. In a large frying pan brown the ground beef, onion and garlic. Drain off fat.
2. In a large soup pot combine the beef mixture with all the remaining ingredients. Bring to a boil. Reduce heat, cover and simmer for 2 hours.

Shepherd's Pie

1 pound	ground beef
¼ cup	chopped onion
1 can	(10 oz.) condensed vegetable soup
¼ teaspoon	salt
2 cups	mashed potatoes (3 large potatoes)
	Melted butter

There are many variations on this classic recipe which produces a hearty and inexpensive meal.

1. Combine ground beef and onion in skillet and cook until beef is browned. Drain fat, stir in soup and salt.
2. Spoon into a 1 quart casserole dish. Spoon potatoes evenly over top. Brush with melted butter. Bake at 425° F. for 15 to 20 minutes. Makes 4 servings.

Dad's Deluxe Meat Loaf

1 can	(10 oz.) beef gravy
1½ pounds	ground beef
1 cup	small bread cubes
1	egg, slightly beaten
¼ cup	minced onion
1 teaspoon	salt
	Dash of pepper
1 can	(8 oz.) Pillsbury crescent rolls

Dad wrote this recipe out - I don't remember where from, but it quickly became a family favourite.

1. Combine 1/4 cup gravy with the ground beef, bread cubes, egg, onion, salt and pepper. Shape firmly into a 7 x 5 inch loaf. Place in a shallow baking dish. Bake at 375° F. for 45 minutes.
2. Separate crescent rolls and place crosswise over top and down sides of the loaf, overlapping slightly. Bake 15 minutes more. Heat the remaining gravy to serve with the meat loaf.

Beef and Noodle Casserole

2 cups	cooked egg noodles
1 pound	ground beef
1 can	(15 oz.) tomato sauce
1 - 2 cloves	garlic, minced
	Salt and pepper
1 package	(4 oz.) cream cheese, softened
1 cup	sour cream
2	green onions, chopped
1 cup	grated Cheddar cheese

A quick and easy casserole - very tasty and attractive too, with all the colourful layers! The recipe can be doubled to serve a larger crowd.

1. Spread cooked noodles in the bottom of a medium casserole dish (2 quart). In a frying pan brown ground beef and garlic. Drain and discard fat.
2. Add tomato sauce to the meat, heat and simmer for 15 minutes. Season with salt and pepper to taste. Pour meat mixture over the noodles in casserole dish.
3. In a small bowl combine the cream cheese with the sour cream and mix until smooth. Stir in green onions. Spread over meat mixture. Sprinkle Cheddar cheese over top of the cream cheese. Bake, uncovered, at 350° F. for 35 minutes. Makes about 4 servings.

Ground Beef Porcupines

1 pound	ground beef
½ cup	uncooked regular rice
½ cup	water
⅓ cup	chopped onion
1 teaspoon	salt
½ teaspoon	celery salt
⅛ teaspoon	garlic powder
⅛ teaspoon	pepper
1 can	(15 oz.) tomato sauce
1 cup	water
2 teaspoons	Worchestershire sauce

Meatballs with "something extra." The rice pops up during cooking to make the meatballs look like little porcupines! Kids will love them. Serve with rice.

1. Mix ground beef, rice, 1/2 cup water, onion, and seasonings together. Scoop out rounded tablespoonfuls and form into meatballs. Arrange meatballs in a single layer in an 8 inch square baking dish.

2. Stir together the tomato sauce, 1 cup water and Worchestershire sauce. Pour over the meatballs. Cover the dish with aluminum foil and bake at 350° F. for 45 minutes. Uncover and bake for another 15 minutes. Makes 4 to 6 servings.

Sweet and Sour Meatballs

MEATBALLS:

2 pounds	ground beef
1 package	dry onion soup mix
½ cup	oatmeal
1	egg

SAUCE:

3 tablespoons	cornstarch
¾ cup	ketchup
2 cups	water
½ cup	vinegar
¾ cup	sugar

Very yummy - kids love these. Also great for potluck meals. Serve over rice. I usually add some Worchestershire sauce to the sweet and sour sauce.

1. MEATBALLS: Mix all ingredients together and form into meatballs. Arrange in a single row in a baking dish. Bake, covered, at 350° F. for 30 minutes. Remove from oven and drain fat from the dish.

2. SAUCE: Combine all ingredients in a saucepan and boil for 10 to 15 minutes. Pour over baked meatballs. Cover and return to the oven for 45 minutes to 1 hour. Makes 6 servings.

Tourtiere

1	large potato
1 pound	lean ground beef
1 pound	lean ground pork
1	medium onion, chopped
1½ teaspoons	salt
½ teaspoon	thyme
½ teaspoon	sage
½ teaspoon	dry mustard
¼ teaspoon	cloves
	Pastry for two 9 inch pies

This French Canadian classic meat pie is traditionally served for dinner on Christmas Eve.

1. Boil and mash potato, saving 1/2 cup potato water. Set potato aside. Mix all other ingredients, except pastry, with reserved potato water in a heavy saucepan. Bring to a boil and simmer, covered, for 40 minutes. Remove from heat and add mashed potato. Mix well and chill.

2. Pour cooled meat mixture into 2 pastry lined pie plates. Cover with top crust and seal edges. Slash top to allow steam to escape. Bake at 425° F. for 25 minutes. Makes 12 servings.

Ground Beef Casserole

2 pounds	ground beef
2 cups	chopped celery
2 cups	chopped onion
1 can	(10 oz.) mushrooms, drained
1 can	(10 oz.) tomato soup
1 can	(10 oz.) cream of mushroom soup
1 cup	water
1 can	Chow Mein noodles
	Salt and pepper

A prairie classic - popular for potluck suppers. Great for family suppers too, especially on a cold winter night. Leftovers can be frozen.

1. In a large skillet, combine the ground beef, celery and onions. Cook until meat is browned and vegetables are soft. Drain excess fat. Add mushrooms, soups and water and stir to combine.

2. Reserve 1/2 cup of the Chow Mein noodles and add the rest to the ground beef mixture. Season with salt and pepper. Turn into a large casserole dish and top with the reserved Chow Mein noodles. Bake at 350° F. for 45 minutes. Makes 6 to 8 servings.

Homesteader Beef Pie

1 pound	ground beef
½ cup	chopped onion
1 can	(5 ½ oz.) tomato paste
½ teaspoon	salt
¼ teaspoon	Italian seasoning
	Dash of pepper
1 can	(8 oz.) Pillsbury crescent rolls
6	process cheese slices

We made this back home when I was young and thought it was really fancy! Kids will love it - and adults too (who doesn't love those Pillsbury crescent rolls?) It is very filling, add a salad, and you'll be set.

1. In a medium frying pan brown the ground beef. Add the onion and cook until tender. Drain off fat. Stir in tomato paste and seasonings.

2. Lightly grease a 9 inch pie pan. Separate the crescent dough into 8 triangles. Place in the pie pan, pressing the triangles together, to form a crust.

3. Fill with half of the meat mixture. Top with 3 cheese slices, then the rest of the meat.

4. Bake at 375° F. for 25 minutes, until the crust is golden brown.

5. Cut each of the remaining 3 cheese slices into 4 lengthwise strips. Arrange the strips over the pie to form a lattice. Return to the oven until the cheese melts. Makes 4 to 6 servings.

Pork

Spanish Style Chops

1 tablespoon	oil
½ teaspoon	chili powder
2 cloves	garlic, crushed
4	pork chops, ¾ inch thick
1 cup	long grain rice
1 cup	chopped celery
1 cup	chopped green pepper
½ cup	chopped onion
½ teaspoon	salt
¼ teaspoon	pepper
2 cups	tomato juice
1 cup	water

An easy to prepare casserole combining pork chops and Spanish rice.

1. Combine oil, chili powder, and garlic. Rub chops on both sides with the spiced oil mixture, and let stand for about 15 minutes.

2. In an 8 cup baking dish, combine rice, celery, green pepper, onion, salt and pepper. Stir to mix it all together. Arrange chops on top of the rice mixture.

3. Mix tomato juice and water, and pour over all. Cover and bake at 325° F. for 1 hour. Makes 4 servings.

Swiss Pork Chops and Vegetables

4	pork chops, ¾ inch thick
4	potatoes, halved
4	onions
4	large carrots, peeled
1 cup	beef broth
1 can	(5 ½ oz.) tomato paste
¼ cup	brown sugar
½ teaspoon	dry mustard
1 teaspoon	Italian seasoning
2	bay leaves

Can't get much easier than this, very little preparation time is required, your meal is in the oven, and you can go on to other things while it bakes.

1. Put pork chops in an 8 or 9 inch casserole dish. Place vegetables on top.

2. Mix remaining ingredients together, and pour over the meat and vegetables. Cover and bake at 375° F. for 1 hour to 1 hour 15 minutes. Remove the bay leaves. Makes 4 servings.

Pork and Yam Bake

6	thick loin pork chops
2 tablespoons	oil
6	small - medium yams
1 can	(14 oz.) crushed pineapple
	Salt and pepper
2 teaspoons	orange rind
3 tablespoons	honey
2 tablespoons	butter

A simple casserole combining pork chops with the tasty tropical combination of yams (or sweet potatoes) and pineapple.

1. Heat oil in a large frying pan. Brown chops. Peel and thinly slice yams. Place in bottom of a casserole dish. Drain pineapple and reserve juice. Spread pineapple over yams. Top with pork chops. Season with salt and pepper.

2. Heat pineapple juice, orange rind, honey and butter. Pour over pork chops. Cover and bake at 350° F. for 45 minutes. Check liquid and add water if necessary. Bake another 20 minutes. Makes 6 servings.

Pineapple Pork

1 pound	pork, cut in 1 inch cubes
1	medium onion, chopped
1 tablespoon	oil
2 tablespoons	brown sugar
2 tablespoons	cornstarch
	Salt and pepper
2 tablespoons	vinegar
2 tablespoons	soy sauce
⅓ cup	ketchup
⅓ cup	water
1 can	(19 oz.) pineapple cubes
1	green pepper, cut in strips

Serve this delicious sweet and sour dish over rice.

1. Brown pork and onion in oil.

2. Combine sugar, cornstarch, salt and pepper. Add vinegar, soy sauce, ketchup, water and juice drained from pineapple. Stir until smooth. Add to the browned meat, cook and stir until thick and clear. Cover and simmer 1 hour.

3. Add pineapple cubes and green pepper and cook 5 minutes to heat through. Makes 4 servings.

Barbecued Pork Pot Roast

2½ pound	pork shoulder roast (skin off)
	Dry mustard
	Salt, pepper and sage
2 tablespoons	oil
1	diced onion
½ cup	apple sauce
½ cup	barbecue sauce or ketchup
½ teaspoon	garlic powder
2 tablespoons	steak sauce

Everyday ingredients combine to make a very flavourful sauce for this pork roast.

1. Rub meat with dry mustard, salt, pepper and sage. Heat oil in frying pan. Brown meat on all sides. Place in roasting pan.

2. Mix remaining ingredients together and pour over top of the meat. Cover and bake at 300° F. for 2 1/2 to 3 hours, turning 2 - 3 times. Makes 6 servings.

Pork Chop Casserole

6	pork chops (1 inch thick)
5 cups	thinly sliced potatoes
1 cup	chopped onion
1 can	(10 oz.) cream of mushroom soup
1 cup	milk
1 teaspoon	sage
	Salt and pepper

Pork chops and scalloped potatoes, all in one dish - easy!

1. Brown pork chops on both sides. In a greased 9 x 13 inch pan, layer half of the potatoes. Top with half of the onions, then the remaining potatoes and onions. Arrange the pork chops on top.

2. Mix mushroom soup, milk, sage, salt and pepper. Pour over the pork chops. Cover and bake at 350° F. for 1 hour. Makes 6 servings.

Italian Pork Chops

6	thick pork chops
2 tablespoons	oil
1 cup	tomato sauce
¼ cup	green olives, chopped
1	green pepper, chopped
1 can	(10 oz.) mushrooms, drained

A simple combination of pork chops and tomato sauce.

1. Brown chops in oil. Drain excess fat. Add tomato sauce, olives and green pepper. Bring to a boil, reduce heat, cover and simmer for 1 hour.

2. Add mushroooms and cook 5 minutes to heat through. Makes 6 servings.

Baked Pork Chops and Apples

6	thick pork chops
	Salt and pepper
4	apples, cored but unpeeled, sliced
4	medium onions, sliced
½ cup	brown sugar
1 tablespoon	cinnamon
2 tablespoons	butter
	Juice of 1 lemon
¼ cup	water

Pork chops and apples go so well together in this simple and tasty dish.

1. Season pork chops with salt and pepper. Brown. Arrange apple and onion slices in a deep casserole.

2. Mix brown sugar and cinnamon together. Sprinkle 3/4 of this over the apples and onions. Place browned pork chops on top. Sprinkle remaining brown sugar mixture over chops.

3. Heat butter, lemon juice and water together. Pour over all. Cover and bake at 325° F. for 50 minutes. Uncover and bake for another 10 minutes. Makes 6 servings.

Barbecue Pork Chops

6	thick pork chops
½ cup	ketchup
1 teaspoon	celery seed
⅓ cup	vinegar
1 teaspon	salt
½ teaspoon	nutmeg
1 cup	water

A classic combination of pork chops and barbecue style sauce.

1. Brown chops. Place in a shallow baking dish.

2. Mix remaining ingredients to make sauce. Pour sauce over pork chops. Bake at 350° F. for 1 1/2 hours. Turn twice and baste with sauce. Makes 6 servings.

Pork and Sweet Potato Stew

⅓ cup	brown sugar
⅓ cup	flour
¼ cup	Dijon mustard
3 pounds	pork, cut in 1 inch cubes
3 tablespoons	olive oil
1	onion, chopped
2 cloves	garlic, minced
1⅓ cups	chicken broth
1 cup	dry sherry
3 pounds	sweet potatoes, peeled and cut in 1 inch cubes
	Salt and pepper
¼ cup	fresh parsley, chopped

This is a very tasty casserole that is fancy enough for company - serve it with crusty rolls or bread to soak up the delicious sauce.

1. Combine brown sugar and flour in a small bowl. Coat pork cubes in mustard, then in the flour mixture. Heat oil in a large frying pan, and brown pork cubes on all sides. Transfer pork cubes to a large casserole dish. Continue until all pork cubes are browned. Add onion and garlic to the frying pan and cook until softened but not brown. Add them to the casserole dish.

2. Discard any fat in the frying pan. Add the broth and sherry to the pan, and bring to a boil. Pour into the casserole dish. Add sweet potato cubes to the casserole dish. Cover and bake at 350° F. for 50 to 60 minutes, until meat and sweet potatoes are tender. Season with salt and pepper to taste, and add parsley. Makes 8 servings.

Poultry

Chicken Cacciatore

2 pounds	chicken parts
¼ cup	flour
2 tablespoons	olive oil
1	onion, chopped
2 cloves	garlic, minced
1	green pepper, sliced
1 cup	mushrooms, sliced
3	tomatoes, peeled and chopped
1 can	(5 ½ oz.) tomato paste
¼ cup	white wine
½ cup	chicken stock
1	bay leaf
1 teaspoon	basil
	Salt and freshly ground pepper

A hearty Italian style classic. Good served with pasta. A 19 ounce can of tomatoes, drained, can be used in place of fresh tomatoes.

1. Coat chicken parts with flour. Heat oil in a large pan and cook the chicken until golden brown all over - about 10 minutes. Add the onion, garlic, green pepper and mushrooms and cook for 3 more minutes.

2. Drain excess fat from the pan. Add the remaining ingredients. Cover and simmer over low heat for 30 to 40 minutes, until the chicken is tender. Remove bay leaf and serve. Makes 4 servings.

Microwave Chicken and Dressing

1 package	herb stuffing mix
2 - 3 pounds	chicken pieces
1 can	(10 oz.) cream of celery soup
	Freshly ground pepper

Sunday "roast chicken" in minutes! If you use boneless skinless chicken breasts they will only need 12 to 15 minutes cooking time.

1. Prepare stuffing mix according to the package directions. Spread in the bottom of a microwave baking dish. Top with chicken pieces. Spread soup over top, and grind pepper over.

2. Cover with waxed paper and cook in the microwave, on high, for 20 to 25 minutes. Let stand 5 minutes. Makes 4 to 6 servings.

Chicken Delight

1 cup	uncooked rice
1	fryer chicken, cut up
1 package	dry onion soup mix
1 can	(10 oz.) cream of chicken soup
1 soup can	water
1 can	sliced mushrooms, drained
	Paprika
	Salt and pepper

This is an old recipe from "back home", for a super easy casserole. The few simple pantry ingredients add up to a tasty meal. You can use 2 - 3 pounds of chicken parts instead of a whole cut up chicken.

1. Place rice in a large greased flat casserole dish. Arrange chicken pieces on top.
2. In a saucepan mix onion soup mix, chicken soup, water and mushrooms. Heat, and pour over chicken. Top with paprika, salt and pepper. Cover and bake at 350° F. for 1 1/2 to 2 hours. Remove lid for the last 15 minutes to brown. Makes 6 servings.

Island Style Chicken

2 pounds	chicken parts
2 tablespoons	oil
1 can	(8 oz.) pineapple chunks
1 cup	chicken broth
½ cup	vinegar
2 tablespoons	brown sugar
2 teaspoons	soy sauce
1 clove	garlic, minced
1	medium green pepper, cut up
3 tablespoons	cornstarch
¼ cup	water

An excellent sweet and sour chicken recipe - serve it over rice.

1. In a skillet, brown chicken in oil. Pour off fat. Add juice from pineapple, broth, vinegar, sugar, soy sauce and garlic. Cover and cook over low heat for 30 minutes.
2. Add green pepper and pineapple chunks and cook another 5 minutes.
3. Combine cornstarch and water, and gradually stir into the sauce. Cook, stirring, until thickened. Makes 4 servings.

Chicken Parmesan

4 - 6	chicken breasts, boned and skinned
3 tablespoons	olive oil
⅓ cup	bread crumbs
½ cup	grated Parmesan cheese
1	egg, beaten
¾ cup	chopped onion
1 can	(15 oz.) tomato sauce
¼ teaspoon	salt
¼ teaspoon	pepper
1 teaspoon	dried oregano
¼ pound	thinly sliced mozzarella cheese

A tasty chicken recipe - serve it with pasta. Also good as a sandwich in a crusty Italian roll.

1. Combine bread crumbs and Parmesan cheese. Heat 2 tablespoons of oil in a large frying pan. Dip chicken pieces in beaten egg, then in the bread crumb mixture. Cook to brown on both sides - about 5 to 7 minutes.

2. Meanwhile in a saucepan heat the remaining tablespoon of oil, and saute the onion until tender. Stir in the tomato sauce, salt, pepper and oregano. Bring to a boil.

3. Place the chicken pieces in a baking dish. Pour 3/4 of the sauce over top. Arrange the mozzarella slices over top, and pour the remaining sauce over all. Bake, uncovered, at 350° F. for about 20 minutes, until chicken is cooked and cheese is melted. Makes 4 to 6 servings.

Chicken Schnitzel

½ cup	fine dry breadcrumbs
¼ cup	freshly grated Parmesan cheese
¼ teaspoon	Italian seasoning
¼ teaspoon	basil
	Salt
	Freshly ground pepper
1	egg
2 tablespoons	water
6	chicken breasts, skinned and boned
2 tablespoons	butter
2 tablespoons	oil

Very tasty breaded chicken breasts. Serve with pasta and sauce, or with your choice of vegetables.

1. Mix bread crumbs, Parmesan cheese and spices together in a bowl. In another bowl, beat the egg and water together.

2. Dip one piece of chicken in the egg and then in the bread crumb mixture to coat on both sides. Remove to a plate. Continue with all the chicken pieces.

3. Heat the butter and oil together in a large frying pan over medium high heat. Add chicken in a single layer. Do in batches if it will not all fit in your pan. Cook until golden brown on both sides, about 7 to 8 minutes. Remove to a serving platter. Makes 6 servings.

Crispy Sour Cream Chicken

2 - 3 pounds   chicken pieces

MOIST COATING:
½ cup   sour cream
1 tablespoon   lemon juice
1 teaspoon   salt
1 teaspoon   Worchestershire sauce
½ teaspoon   garlic powder
½ teaspoon   celery salt
½ teaspoon   dry mustard
⅛ teaspoon   pepper

DRY COATING:
¾ cup   corn flake crumbs

Forget about deep fried take-out chicken - this is great! Good served with mashed potatoes and biscuits - it's good cold for a picnic too, with salads.

1. Mix moist coating ingredients together in a large bowl. Add chicken pieces and toss to coat. Cover and refrigerate for at least 30 minutes or up to 24 hours if time permits.

2. Roll chicken pieces in corn flake crumbs to coat. Spread out in a foil lined baking pan. Bake at 350° F. for about 45 minutes. Makes 4 to 6 servings.

Chicken With Spanish Rice

2 tablespoons	butter
2	onions, sliced
1 cup	water
2 cloves	garlic, crushed
1 can	(28 oz.) stewed tomatoes
½ cup	pitted black olives, sliced in half
½ teaspoon	leaf oregano
½ teaspoon	basil
½ teaspoon	salt
	Freshly ground pepper
1 cup	long grain rice
4	chicken breasts, skinned
3 tablespoons	freshly grated Parmesan cheese

An excellent chicken casserole. You can also make it with boneless chicken breasts - 45 minutes will be enough baking time if you do this.

1. Melt butter in a large frying pan. Add onion slices and saute until soft, about 5 minutes.

2. Add all the remaining ingredients, except for the rice, chicken and cheese. Break the tomatoes into bite size pieces. Bring the mixture to a boil.

3. Pour into a 2 1/2 quart casserole, and stir in the rice. Arrange chicken on top, skin side up. Cover and bake at 350° F. for 45 to 55 minutes.

4. Preheat broiler. Sprinkle cheese over the chicken. Broil 2 to 3 minutes. Makes 4 servings.

Chicken with Sweet Potato Dressing

4	boneless, skinless chicken breasts
	Salt and pepper
2 tablespoons	olive oil
1	onion, chopped
2 cups	peeled, cubed sweet potato
2 cups	chopped fresh mushrooms
2 teaspoons	dried sage
2 tablespoons	flour
2 cups	chicken stock
¼ cup	cider vinegar
2 teaspoons	Dijon mustard

Chicken breasts cooked with a delicious "dressing" of sweet potatoes, mushrooms and onions - makes a very tasty meal.

1. Season chicken with salt and pepper. Heat oil in a large, wide saucepan and brown chicken on both sides. Remove chicken and add onion, sweet potato, mushrooms and sage to pan. Cook and stir about 5 minutes until the onion is softened. Add up to 1/4 cup of water if required to keep from sticking.

2. Sprinkle flour over vegetables and cook and stir for 1 minute. Stir in stock, vinegar and mustard, and bring to a boil. Return chicken to the pan. Cover and simmer for 20 minutes, until chicken and sweet potatoes are cooked. Makes 4 servings.

Chicken Dijon Stew

4 cups	brussels sprouts
2 pounds	skinless boneless chicken breasts
3 tablespoons	olive oil
½ pound	baby carrots, peeled
½ cup	white wine
1 can	(10 oz.) cream of chicken soup
2 tablespoons	Dijon mustard
2 teaspoons	dried tarragon
	Freshly ground pepper

This quick and easy recipe is elegant enough to serve to company. You can substitute parsley or cilantro for the tarragon if desired. The sauce is really tasty - serve with fresh bread or crusty rolls to soak it up.

1. Prepare and cook brussels sprouts until just tender. Drain and set aside.

2. Cut chicken into 1 1/2 inch cubes. Heat oil in a large saucepan. Add chicken, brussels sprouts, and carrots. Cook and stir over medium high heat until chicken is lightly browned, about 5 minutes.

3. Add wine, soup, mustard, tarragon, and pepper. Stir to blend. Heat to boiling. Reduce heat to low, cover and simmer until chicken is cooked through, about 10 minutes. Stir occasionally. Makes 6 servings.

Leftover Turkey Casserole

2 cans	(10 oz. each) mushroom soup
1 can	(10 oz.) sliced mushrooms
1 cup	chopped onion
1 cup	chopped celery
	Salt and pepper
¼ cup	juice from mushrooms
2 cups	cooked turkey, cut in small pieces
1 can	Chow Mein noodles

This was my Mom's favourite for leftover holiday turkey. If you have too much turkey, you can make this and freeze it for later. In that case, don't bake it first - thaw and bake when you want to serve it.

1. Reserve 1/4 of the chow mein noodles. Mix everything else together, and pour into a casserole dish.

2. Top with the reserved Chow Mein noodles. Bake, uncovered, at 325° F. for 40 minutes. Makes 4 to 6 servings.

Seafood

Shrimp Creole Casserole

1 pound	large cooked shrimp (peeled and deveined)
2 tablespoons	lemon juice
2 tablespoons	olive oil
¾ cup	long grain rice
¼ cup	finely chopped onion
¼ cup	finely chopped green pepper
⅛ teaspoon	mace
¼ teaspoon	hot sauce
	Salt and pepper
1 can	(10 oz.) tomato soup
½ cup	whipping cream
½ cup	sherry
½ cup	toasted slivered almonds
	Paprika

A very easy and attractive dish to make for company or to take for a potluck dinner. It has a really nice mellow taste.

1. Place shrimp in a large bowl. Add lemon juice and olive oil and toss to coat. Set aside. Cook rice according to package directions.

2. Put onion and green pepper in a small dish and microwave on high for about 4 minutes, until softened. (You can saute them in butter on the stove instead.)

3. Add cooked rice and onions and green peppers to the shrimp. Add seasonings, soup, cream and sherry to the shrimp mixture and stir to combine. Spoon into a 2 quart casserole. Top with almonds and paprika. Bake uncovered at 350° F. for 70 minutes. Makes 6 servings.

Salmon Loaf

2 cans	(7 oz. each) salmon
1 cup	dry breadcrumbs
¼ cup	milk
¼ cup	butter
3	large eggs, separated
1 tablespoon	lemon juice
1 tablespoon	grated onion
2 tablespoons	chopped parsley
½ teaspoon	Worchestershire sauce
¼ teaspoon	salt
⅛ teaspoon	pepper

You can use red, or the less expensive pink salmon to make this very tasty salmon loaf.

1. Drain salmon, and reserve liquid. Pour reserved salmon liquid over breadcrumbs in a large bowl.

2. Heat milk and butter together until butter is barely melted. Add to the breadcrumbs. Flake and add salmon. Stir in egg yolks, lemon juice, onion, parsley, Worchestershire sauce, salt and pepper.

3. Beat egg whites until stiff. Fold into salmon mixture. Pour into a greased 8 x 5 inch loaf pan.

4. Place the loaf pan in a shallow pan of boiling water (1 inch deep). Bake at 350° F. for 40 minutes, until firm. Makes 6 servings.

Pasta

Beef and Cheese Pasta

1 package	(10 oz.) spinach
1 tablespoon	oil
1	onion, chopped
2 cloves	garlic, minced
1 teaspoon	thyme
	Salt and pepper
2 cups	sliced mushrooms
1 pound	ground beef
4 cups	small pasta
2 tablespoons	butter
3 tablespoons	flour
2 cups	milk
1½ cups	grated Cheddar cheese
½ teaspoon	salt
½ teaspoon	pepper
¼ teaspoon	nutmeg

A different kind of pasta dish - macaroni and cheese with a meat layer in the middle. And a nice change from the usual meat and tomato sauce with pasta. You can use macaroni, or make it fancier with bowtie or other pasta shapes.

1. Wash spinach and drain well. Cook in a pot with the water clinging to the leaves, just until tender and wilted. Drain and squeeze out any remaining water. Chop and set aside.

2. In a large skillet, heat the oil, and saute the onion and garlic for about 5 minutes. Stir in the thyme, salt and pepper to taste, and the sliced mushrooms. Cook for another 5 minutes. Add the ground beef and cook until no longer pink.

3. Remove from heat and drain any excess fat from the pan. Add the spinach to this mixture. Cook pasta and drain.

4. Melt butter. Stir in flour. Slowly pour in milk while stirring over medium heat. Reduce heat and simmer, stirring, for about 10 minutes until thick.

5. Remove from heat and stir in 1 cup of the cheese, salt, pepper and nutmeg. Mix this cheese sauce together with the pasta until combined.

6. Spoon half of the pasta into a 3 quart casserole dish. Top with the meat mixture and then the remaining pasta. Sprinkle the remaining 1/2 cup of cheese over top. Bake at 375° F. for 25 to 30 minutes. Makes 6 servings.

Lasagna

1 pound	ground beef
1	onion, chopped
½ cup	celery, chopped
2 cloves	garlic, minced
1 can	(13 oz.) tomato paste
1 can	(19 oz.) stewed tomatoes
	Salt and pepper
1	bay leaf
1 tablespoon	parsley
1 teaspoon	basil
1 teaspoon	oregano
1 package	lasagna noodles
2 cups	cottage cheese
2 cups	grated mozzarella cheese
½ cup	grated Parmesan cheese

This is great lasagna! You can add mushrooms to the sauce if desired. If you use fresh lasagna noodles, you can use them in this recipe without cooking. Microwaving keeps it nice and moist, not dried out. But if you want to bake it instead, bake for about 45 minutes at 375° F.

1. In a large skillet, combine beef, onion, celery and garlic. Cook and stir over medium heat until meat is browned, and vegetables softened. Drain fat.

2. Add tomato paste, tomatoes, salt and pepper, bay leaf, parsley, basil and oregano. Bring to a boil, reduce heat and simmer 10 minutes. Remove bay leaf. Cook pasta and drain.

3. In a 9 x 13 inch baking dish layer 1/3 of the meat sauce. Top with 1/2 of the noodles, 1/2 of the cottage cheese, 1/2 of the mozzarella cheese, and 1/3 of the Parmesan cheese. Repeat layers, and end with the remaining meat sauce and Parmesan cheese. Cover with wax paper, microwave on high for 15 to 20 minutes. Let stand a few minutes before serving. Makes 8 servings.

Macaroni and Cheese

2 cups	elbow macaroni
2 tablespoons	butter
2 tablespoons	flour
¾ cup	milk
1 cup	sour cream or plain yogurt
½ cup	finely chopped onion
½ cup	chopped celery
2 cups	grated Cheddar cheese

For classic comfort food, macaroni and cheese has to come out on top.

1. Cook pasta and drain. In a medium saucepan, melt the butter. Stir in the flour, then gradually stir in the milk. Heat and stir until thick.

2. Remove from heat and stir in the sour cream, onion, celery, 1 1/2 cups of the cheese, and the pasta. Put the mixture in a 2 quart casserole dish. Sprinkle the remaining 1/2 cup cheese over top. Bake at 350° F. for 45 minutes. Makes 4 servings.

Macaroni with Salmon

1½ cups	elbow macaroni
3 tablespoons	butter
1	onion, chopped
1 clove	garlic, minced
3 tablespoons	flour
½ teaspoon	Worcestershire sauce
1¾ cups	milk
2 cups	grated Cheddar cheese
1 cup	sour cream or plain yogurt
2 cans	(7 ¾ oz. each) salmon

Salmon makes a great addition to macaroni and cheese, for a complete meal. You can also make this with tuna instead of salmon, or leave it out for "just plain" macaroni and cheese. Use light cheese, skim milk and yogurt to reduce the fat content.

1. Cook pasta and drain. In a large saucepan, melt butter. Add onion and garlic and cook until tender. Stir in the flour and Worcestershire sauce. Gradually stir in milk. Bring to a boil, stirring constantly. Remove from heat. Add 1 1/2 cups of the cheese and stir until melted. Add sour cream.

2. Drain the salmon and break into bite size chunks, discarding skin and bones. Add to the cheese mixture, along with the macaroni. Put the mixture in a 2 quart casserole dish. Sprinkle the remaining 1/2 cup of cheese on top. Bake at 350° F. for 25 to 30 minutes. Makes 6 servings.

Spinach Manicotti

1 package	(10 oz.) spinach
2 cups	ricotta cheese
1½ cups	grated mozzarella cheese
¾ cup	grated Parmesan cheese
¼ cup	finely chopped onion
1	egg
1 teaspoon	parsley
1 clove	garlic, minced
½ teaspoon	pepper
2 jars	(28 oz. each) spaghetti sauce
1½ cups	water
1 package	manicotti shells

The trick is to prepare this the night before - then the manicotti shells don't need to be precooked, which makes it much easier to stuff them.

1. Wash spinach and drain well. Cook in a pot with the water clinging to the leaves, just until tender and wilted. Drain and squeeze out any remaining water. Chop. Combine in a large bowl with the ricotta cheese, 1 cup of the mozzarella cheese, 1/4 cup of the Parmesan cheese, onion, egg, parsley, garlic, and pepper.

2. Combine spaghetti sauce and water. Pour 1 cup of the sauce in the bottom of a 9 x 13 inch pan.

3. Stuff uncooked manicotti shells with the cheese mixture. Place over the sauce in the pan. Pour the remaining sauce over, and top with the remaining mozzarella cheese and Parmesan cheese.

4. Cover and refrigerate overnight. Remove from the refrigerator 30 minutes before putting in the oven. Bake, uncovered, at 350° F. for 40 to 50 minutes. Makes 8 servings.

Party Pasta

2 pounds	ground beef
3 cloves	garlic, minced
2	medium onions, chopped
1 can	(15 oz.) tomato sauce
1 can	(19 oz.) stewed tomatoes
1 can	(10 oz.) sliced mushroom with juice
1 teaspoon	oregano
1 teaspoon	basil
	Salt and pepper
5 cups	shell, rigatoni or other large pasta
2 cups	sour cream or plain yogurt
2 cups	grated Cheddar cheese
2 cups	grated mozzarella cheese

This large pasta recipe is good to make for a party or to take along to a potluck dinner.

1. In a large skillet, combine beef, garlic, and onions. Cook and stir over medium heat until browned. Drain fat. Add tomato sauce, tomatoes, mushrooms, oregano, basil, salt and pepper. Bring to a boil, reduce heat and simmer 20 minutes. Cook pasta and drain.

2. In a 4 quart (or larger) casserole, layer 1/2 of the pasta. Top with the 1/2 of the meat sauce, 1/2 of the sour cream, 1/2 of the Cheddar cheese. Repeat layers and top with the mozzarella cheese. Cover and bake at 350° F. for 45 minutes. Remove cover and continue to bake until cheese is melted. Makes 10 servings.

Tuna Florentine

2 tablespoons	butter
1	medium onion, chopped
1 clove	garlic, minced
1 can	(19 oz.) tomatoes
1 can	(7 ½ oz.) tomato sauce
½ teaspoon	basil
	Salt and pepper
3 cups	medium egg noodles
1 package	(10 oz.) spinach
1 can	(6 ½ oz.) tuna
¼ cup	grated Parmesan cheese

Tuna casserole extraordinaire!

1. Melt the butter in a large skillet. Add onion and garlic and cook until softened. Stir in tomatoes, tomato sauce, basil, salt and pepper. Simmer for 20 minutes. Cook pasta and drain. Wash spinach and drain well. Cook in a pot with the water clinging to the leaves, just until tender and wilted. Drain and squeeze out any remaining water. Chop.

2. Break tuna into chunks and gently stir into the tomato sauce, along with the noodles. Pour into a 2 quart casserole dish. Top with spinach and then sprinkle Parmesan cheese over top. Bake at 375° F. for 25 minutes. Makes 4 servings.

Beefy Macaroni and Cheese

1 pound	ground beef
1	onion, chopped
2 cans	(15 oz. each) tomato sauce
1 cup	water
½ teaspoon	oregano
½ teaspoon	salt
½ cup	pitted ripe olives, sliced
2 cups	elbow macaroni
2 cups	cubed process cheese (e.g. Velveeta)

A nice mellow pasta casserole, really tasty!

1. In a large skillet, brown beef. Add onion and saute until tender. Drain fat. Add tomato sauce, water, oregano, salt and olives. Simmer 10 minutes. Cook pasta and drain.

2. In a 2 1/2 quart casserole dish, layer half of the macaroni. Top with half of the meat sauce, and half of the cheese. Repeat layers. Bake at 375° F. for 20 to 30 minutes. Makes 6 servings.

Baked Pasta

4 cups	penne or other small pasta
1 pound	ground beef
4 cloves	garlic, minced
2	onions, chopped
1 can	(28 oz.) stewed tomatoes
1 tablespoon	brown sugar
1 tablespoon	cumin
1 tablespoon	basil
½ teaspoon	dried chilies
½ teaspoon	Tabasco sauce
½ teaspoon	salt
1 can	(15 oz.) tomato sauce
1 package	(8 oz.) cream cheese
2 cups	grated mozzarella cheese

A spicy pasta casserole, this is a good one to serve a crowd. You can use more or less seasonings to suit your taste.

1. Cook pasta and drain. In a large saucepan, brown the ground beef, garlic and onion. Drain fat. Add tomatoes, brown sugar, and seasonings. Bring to a boil, reduce heat, and simmer 15 minutes. Stir in the tomato sauce and pasta.

2. Cut cream cheese into 1/2 inch cubes and stir into the meat sauce.

3. Put the mixture in a 4 quart casserole dish, or 9 x 13 inch pan. Sprinkle the mozzarella cheese on top. Bake at 350° F. for 30 to 35 minutes. Makes 8 servings.

Creamy Baked Pasta

2 pounds	ground beef
2 cloves	garlic, minced
2 cans	(15 oz. each) tomato sauce
	Salt and pepper
4 cups	macaroni or other small pasta
1 package	(8 oz.) cream cheese, softened
2 cups	sour cream or plain yogurt
½ cup	chopped green onion
2 cups	grated Cheddar cheese

A delicious pasta casserole, very attractive too. You can easily half it for a smaller family dinner.

1. In a large skillet, combine beef and garlic. Cook and stir over medium heat until browned. Drain fat. Add tomato sauce, salt and pepper. Bring to a boil, reduce heat and simmer 15 minutes.

2. Cook pasta and drain. Spread in the bottom of a 4 quart casserole. Top with the meat sauce.

3. In a medium bowl mix the cream cheese and sour cream or yogurt. Blend until smooth. Stir in green onions. Layer over the meat sauce.

4. Top all with the Cheddar cheese. Bake at 350° F. for 35 to 40 minutes, until casserole is heated through. Makes 8 servings.

Pasta Florentine

4 cups	small pasta
1 package	(10 oz.) spinach
2 cups	cottage cheese
½ cup	plain yogurt
¾ cup	grated Parmesan cheese
½ teaspoon	salt
¼ teaspoon	Tabasco sauce
1 teaspoon	basil
½ teaspoon	thyme
1 tablespoon	butter
1 tablespoon	flour
1 cup	boiling chicken broth

A tasty and lower fat (use 1% cottage cheese) meatless pasta meal. Make it fancy with bow-tie or corkscrew pasta. For a larger crowd it is a nice side dish.

1. Cook pasta and drain. Wash spinach and drain well. Cook in a pot with the water clinging to the leaves, just until tender and wilted. Drain and squeeze out any remaining water. Chop. Combine in a large bowl with the cottage cheese, yogurt, 1/2 cup of the Parmesan cheese, salt, Tabasco sauce, basil and thyme. Stir in the pasta.

2. Place in a 1 1/2 quart casserole. Melt butter. Stir in flour. Slowly pour in boiling broth while stirring. Pour sauce over the pasta. Top with remaining Parmesan cheese. Bake at 350° F. for 30 to 35 minutes. Makes 4 to 6 servings.

Baked Rigatoni and Meatballs

MEATBALLS:

1	egg
⅓ cup	onion, chopped
¼ cup	dry bread crumbs
2 cloves	garlic, minced
3 tablespoons	grated Parmesan cheese
1 teaspoon	oregano
	Salt and pepper
1 pound	ground beef

PASTA:

2 tablespoons	olive oil
1	onion, chopped
2 cloves	garlic, minced
3 cups	sliced mushrooms
1	green pepper, chopped
2 teaspoons	basil
1 teaspoon	oregano
	Salt and pepper
1 can	(28 oz.) stewed tomatoes
1 can	(5 ½ oz.) tomato paste
3½ cups	rigatoni pasta
1½ cups	grated mozzarella cheese
¼ cup	grated Parmesan cheese

This is a little more trouble to prepare, but well worth it. If you prefer you can make the meatballs with ground turkey or chicken instead of beef. An attractive dish.

1. MEATBALLS: In a medium bowl, slightly beat egg, add onion, bread crumbs, garlic, Parmesan cheese, oregano, salt and pepper. Mix to combine, then mix in the ground beef. Shape into small meatballs using around a heaping tablespoon of mixture for a meatball.

2. PASTA: Heat oil in a large skillet. Brown meatballs on all sides and remove. Cook in batches if necessary. Drain excess fat from the pan. Add onion, garlic, mushrooms, green pepper, basil, oregano, salt and pepper, plus 2 tablespoons of water. Cook over medium heat about 10 minutes until vegetables are softened. Stir in tomatoes, tomato paste and meatballs. Simmer for 30 minutes.

3. Cook pasta and drain. Add pasta to sauce and stir to combine. Transfer to a 2 1/2 quart casserole dish. Sprinkle the mozzarella cheese on top, then the Parmesan cheese. Bake at 400° F. for 20 minutes. Makes 6 servings.

Spaghetti and Meatballs

MEATBALLS:

1 pound	lean ground beef
½ cup	chopped onion
½ cup	breadcrumbs
¼ cup	grated Parmesan cheese
2	eggs
	Salt and pepper

Very easy and yummy! The meatballs don't need to be browned, they just simmer in the sauce, so use lean beef that won't add a lot of fat.

SAUCE:

1 cup	chopped onion
2 cloves	garlic, minced
½ pound	mushrooms, sliced
1 can	(28 oz.) stewed tomatoes
1 can	(13 oz.) tomato paste
½ cup	red wine
1 teaspoon	parsley
1 teaspoon	oregano
1 teaspoon	basil
	Salt and pepper
1	bay leaf

1. MEATBALLS: Mix all ingredients together. Shape into meatballs. Set aside.
2. SAUCE: Mix all the ingredients together in a large saucepan. Simmer, uncovered, for 20 minutes.
3. Add the meatballs to the sauce. Cover and simmer for 20 to 25 minutes. Remove bay leaf. Serve over spaghetti. Top with Parmesan cheese if desired. Makes 4 servings.

Rigatoni With Sausage Sauce

2 tablespoons	olive oil
1	medium onion, chopped
1	clove garlic, minced
4	Italian sausages
2 cups	mushrooms, sliced
1 tablespoon	basil
¼ cup	red wine
1 can (28 oz.)	tomatoes, drained
¼ cup	milk
	Salt and pepper
	Rigatoni pasta

A tasty pasta sauce. You can use sweet or hot Italian sausages as you prefer. And you can use it with any type of pasta you have on hand too.

1. Heat olive oil in a large saucepan. Add onion and garlic and cook until softened. Remove sausage meat from casing, break up and add to pan. Cook for 5 minutes. Add mushrooms and basil and cook another 5 minutes. Add wine and cook until evaporated. Add tomatoes and simmer 10 minutes. Add milk and salt and pepper to taste.

2. Meanwhile, cook rigatoni pasta. Combine sauce and pasta and place in a serving dish. Serve with Parmesan cheese if desired. Makes 4 servings.

Tomato Sauce

2 tablespoons	olive oil
1	onion, chopped
2 cloves	garlic, minced
8 cups	fresh tomatoes, peeled and chopped
2 teaspoons	basil
1 teaspoon	oregano
1 teaspoon	parsley
	Salt and pepper
1 can	(13 oz.) tomato paste
½ cup	red wine

This is a great recipe to make in the summer with tomatoes fresh from the garden. You can make large batches and freeze in meal size portions.

1. Heat oil in a large pot. Add onion and garlic and cook until soft. Add tomatoes, seasonings, tomato paste and wine. Bring to a boil and simmer, uncovered, for about 30 minutes, until thickened. Remove from heat and serve with pasta, or cool and freeze.

Beef and Sausage Sauce

2 tablespoons	olive oil
2	onions, chopped
3 cloves	garlic, minced
¼ teaspoon	hot pepper flakes (optional)
1 pound	ground beef
1 pound	Italian sausages
4 cups	sliced mushrooms
2 cans	(28 oz. each) stewed tomatoes
1 can	(13 oz.) tomato paste
	Salt and pepper

A good hearty sauce. Use sweet or hot Italian sausages to suit your taste. This sauce can top up any kind of pasta.

1. Heat oil in a large frying pan. Add onions, garlic and hot pepper flakes and cook until softened. Add beef. Remove sausage meat from casings, break up and add to pan. Cook until the meat is browned. Drain off fat. Add mushrooms and cook for 5 minutes.

2. Add tomatoes and tomato paste. Bring to a boil, reduce heat and simmer for 20 to 30 minutes, until thickened. Season with salt and pepper. Serve over pasta. Makes 8 servings.

Bolognese Sauce

2 tablespoons	olive oil
1	onion, chopped
2 cloves	garlic, minced
1 stalk	celery, diced
1	carrot, diced
1 pound	ground beef
3 cups	fresh tomatoes, peeled and chopped
1 teaspoon	basil
1 teaspoon	oregano
1 teaspoon	parsley
2	bay leaves
	Salt and pepper
1 can	(13 oz.) tomato paste
½ cup	beef stock
½ cup	red wine

Another good recipe to "stock up" on when the tomatoes are plentiful. You can multiply the recipe to suit how many tomatoes you have...and the size of your pot!

1. Heat oil in a large pot. Add onion, garlic, celery and carrot. Cook for 5 minutes. Add ground beef and cook until browned. Drain off excess fat.

2. Add remaining ingredients. Bring to a boil and simmer, uncovered, for 1 hour. Remove from heat, remove bay leaves. Serve with pasta, or cool and freeze.

Rigatoni With Chili Sauce

2 tablespoons	oil
1 cup	chopped onion
2 cloves	garlic, minced
1	red or green pepper, chopped
3 tablespoons	chili powder
1 pound	ground beef
1 teaspoon	oregano
1 can	(28 oz.) stewed tomatoes
1 can	(5 ½ oz.) tomato paste
½ cup	red wine
	Salt and pepper
	Rigatoni pasta
	Grated Cheddar cheese and sour cream

Something a little different, also quick and easy - pasta topped with a chili sauce! You can serve this sauce with any pasta you like instead of rigatoni.

1. Heat oil in a large frying pan. Add onion, garlic, pepper and chili powder. Cook and stir until onion is soft. Add ground beef to the pan and cook until the meat is browned. Drain off fat.

2. Add oregano, tomatoes, tomato paste and wine. Bring to a boil, cover and simmer for 10 minutes. Season with salt and pepper to taste.

3. Meanwhile, cook rigatoni pasta. Serve sauce over pasta. Top with Cheddar cheese and a spoonful of sour cream if desired. Makes 4 to 6 servings.

Extra Recipes

Salads & Side Dishes

Salads

Mandarin Almond Salad

⅔ cup	white wine vinegar
1 teaspoon	tarragon leaves
1 tablespoon	honey
½ teaspoon	Dijon mustard
	Salt and freshly ground pepper
½ cup	vegetable oil
1 head	romaine lettuce
1 cup	chopped celery
1 tablespoon	minced parsley
4	green onions, sliced
1 can	(10 oz.) mandarin oranges, drained
½ cup	toasted sliced almonds

A nice refreshing salad. You can prepare the salad dressing early in the day, or even a day or two before serving, and store it in the refrigerator. Add it to the salad immediately before serving.

1. Prepare dressing: in a small bowl mix vinegar, tarragon, honey, mustard, and salt and pepper. Whisk with a wire whisk to combine. Slowly add oil while continuing to whisk. Mix to blend well.
2. In a large bowl, tear the lettuce into bite sized pieces. Add the celery, parsley, onions and mandarin oranges. Toss to combine. Drizzle the dressing over the salad, and sprinkle the almonds over top.

Waldorf Salad

1	green apple (Granny Smith)
2	red apples
1 tablespoon	lemon juice
1 cup	diced celery
1 cup	seedless grapes, halved
¼ cup	mayonnaise
¼ cup	whipping cream
½ cup	coarsely chopped toasted walnuts

A classic salad, fancy enough for special occasions and for potluck meals, but simple enough for every day. You can use light mayonnaise and yogurt instead of whipping cream for a lower fat version.

1. Core and dice apples. Sprinkle with lemon juice. Add celery and grapes to the apples and toss.
2. Combine mayonnaise and cream. Pour over apple mixture and toss to combine. Refrigerate until serving time. It can be served right away or made a few hours in advance. Just before serving add walnuts and toss to mix.

Spicy Coleslaw

6 cups	shredded cabbage
1	small onion, grated
1	carrot, peeled and grated
1 tablespoon	minced parsley
¼ cup	vegetable oil
3 tablespoons	cider vinegar
¼ cup	salad dressing (Miracle Whip)
1 tablespoon	sugar
¼ teaspoon	dry mustard
⅛ teaspoon	garlic powder
½ teaspoon	celery seed
	Salt and freshly ground pepper

A tasty creamy coleslaw recipe. For a quick salad, toss this dressing with a pack of precut coleslaw vegetables from the supermarket.

1. Toss cabbage, onion, carrot and parsley until well mixed. In a small bowl mix the oil, vinegar, salad dressing, sugar and seasonings. Stir to mix well. Pour the dressing over the cabbage mixture and toss gently to mix. Chill for at least 2 hours before serving.

Marinated Coleslaw

12 cups	shredded cabbage (1 medium head)
1	medium onion, chopped
2	carrots, shredded
1	red or green pepper, chopped
1 cup	sugar
1 cup	vinegar
¾ cup	vegetable oil
2 teaspoons	sugar
1 teaspoon	dry mustard
1 teaspoon	celery seed
1 teaspoon	salt

This tangy coleslaw is good to make for a picnic or outdoor get together, because it doesn't contain mayonnaise which can spoil if not kept cold.

1. In a large bowl, combine cabbage, onion, carrots and pepper. Sprinkle with sugar, and set aside. In a small saucepan, combine remaining ingredients. Bring to a boil, remove from heat and pour over vegetables, stirring to cover evenly. Cover and refrigerate overnight. Stir well before serving.

Cauliflower Salad

1	medium cauliflower
2	medium green peppers
8	small tomatoes
¾ cup	white vinegar
½ cup	vegetable oil
2 teaspoons	salt
½ teaspoon	freshly ground pepper

A simple salad with a colourful combination of vegetables.

1. Cut cauliflower into small florets. Steam until tender-crisp. Cut green peppers into strips. Dice tomatoes. Combine cauliflower, pepper strips and tomato together in a bowl. Add the vinegar, oil, salt and pepper. Stir gently to mix. Chill for at least 30 minutes before serving.

Chicken Salad

2½ pounds	chicken pieces
2 cups	chicken broth
1½ cups	mayonnaise
¾ cup	yogurt
2 tablespoons	red wine vinegar
2 teaspoons	Dijon mustard
¼ cup	olive oil
	Salt and pepper
½	red pepper, finely chopped
½	green pepper, finely chopped
1	apple, cored and chopped
2 stalks	celery, finely chopped
1	small red onion, finely chopped

This makes a great chicken salad sandwich, or serve scoops over salad greens as a main course salad.

1. Put chicken in a large saucepan. Add chicken broth. Bring to a boil and simmer over low heat for 35 to 45 minutes. Remove chicken from pan and allow to cool. Discard the skin and bones. Chop the chicken meat into small pieces, and place in a large bowl.

2. In a small bowl, combine the mayonnaise, yogurt, vinegar, mustard and olive oil. Mix well. Season with salt and pepper to taste.

3. Add peppers, apple, celery, and onion to the bowl with the chicken. Pour the mayonnaise mixture over and toss to combine. Chill for several hours or overnight.

Pineapple Chicken Salad

2 pounds	chicken pieces
2 cups	chicken broth
1 cup	diced pineapple
2 stalks	celery, sliced diagonally
1 cup	mayonnaise
2 tablespoons	light cream
½ teaspoon	celery salt
¼ teaspoon	pepper
½ cup	toasted sliced almonds

This is an easy and tasty chicken salad recipe. You can also make it with leftover cooked chicken or turkey.

1. Put chicken in a large saucepan. Add chicken broth. Bring to a boil and simmer over low heat for 35 to 45 minutes. Remove chicken from pan and allow to cool. Discard the skin and bones. Chop the chicken meat into small pieces, and place in a large bowl. Add the pineapple and celery.
2. In a small bowl, combine the mayonnaise, cream, celery salt and pepper. Add the mayonnaise mixture to the chicken and toss to combine. Chill for at least 30 minutes. Sprinkle almonds over top just before serving.

Corn Salad

2 cups	cooked corn kernels
½ cup	chopped green pepper
½ cup	chopped celery
¼ cup	chopped onion
¼ cup	chopped pimento
¼ cup	vegetable oil
3 tablespoons	vinegar
½ teaspoon	salt
¼ teaspoon	pepper
¾ teaspoon	dry mustard

For the "ultimate" corn salad, make this with fresh corn. For a fast salad, use canned corn kernels. You can also use cooked frozen corn.

1. Combine corn, green pepper, celery, onion and pimento together in a large bowl.
2. In a small bowl mix the oil, vinegar and seasonings. Stir to mix well. Pour the dressing over the corn mixture and toss gently to mix. Chill for at least 2 hours before serving.

Grandma's Salad Dressing

1 cup	sugar
2 tablespoons	flour
1	heaping teaspoon mustard powder
1 teaspoon	salt
3	beaten eggs
1 cup	water
½ cup	vinegar

We always had this dressing on hand at home - Mom would make it and store in a jar in the fridge. She said "this is the only dressing that will do for potato salad and devilled eggs."

1. Combine all ingredients in a saucepan. Cook and stir over medium heat until thickened. Remove from heat and cool. Store in the refrigerator.

2. Use to make devilled eggs, or mashed potato salad. To use as a dressing for a green salad, you can add milk to thin it before use if you wish.

Mashed Potato Salad

4 cups	cooked potatoes
3	hard cooked eggs
½ cup	diced radishes
3 - 4	green onions, chopped
½ - 1 cup	Grandma's Salad Dressing, or Miracle Whip
	Paprika

This is the potato salad we always had at home - my Grandma made it, and my Mom and my Aunt too. For years I didn't know that there was "another kind" of potato salad made with cubes of potato.

1. Mash potatoes and eggs. Add radishes and onions. Add enough salad dressing to moisten. Refrigerate for several hours or overnight. Sprinkle paprika over top before serving. You can also garnish with additional sliced egg or radishes.

3 Bean Salad

1 can	(10 oz.) green beans
1 can	(10 oz.) yellow beans
1 can	(14 oz.) kidney beans
½	green pepper, chopped
1	medium Spanish onion, chopped
¾ cup	sugar
⅔ cup	white vinegar
⅓ cup	vegetable oil
1 teaspoon	salt
1 teaspoon	pepper
½ teaspoon	celery salt
Dash	cayenne

We made this salad all the time when I was a kid - it was always one of our favourites. The recipe is from my friend Sharon's mom, Jenny Gerow.

1. Drain beans. Combine in a large bowl with green pepper and onion.
2. Make dressing: in a small saucepan combine the sugar, vinegar, oil and seasonings. Bring to a boil over medium heat to melt the sugar. Pour dressing over the beans and toss to mix all together. Refrigerate for several hours or overnight.

Italian Pasta Salad

3 cups	rotini pasta
1 cup	grated Parmesan cheese
1 cup	Italian salad dressing
½	red pepper, chopped
½	red onion, sliced
2 cups	broccoli, cut into small flowerets
½ cup	black olives, sliced

This is an extremely easy and versatile salad recipe. It is also really good! Tri-color rotini makes the salad very attractive, but you can use any kind of pasta. And add any kind of vegetables too instead of the suggestions here - whatever you have in the fridge. If you have leftover chicken or ham, chop and add that too, then you've got a whole meal.

1. Cook the pasta and drain. Combine the pasta with all the remaining ingredients. Mix together. Chill.

Salads & Side Dishes - Salads

Dilled Salmon Pasta Salad

4 cups	farfalle (bowtie) pasta
2 cans	(7 ½ oz. each) salmon
1 cup	frozen peas
3 - 4	green onions, chopped
⅓ cup	mayonnaise
½ cup	yogurt
2 tablespoons	fresh dill weed (or 2 teaspoons dried)

A quick and easy pasta salad, you don't even have to thaw or cook the peas, just add them frozen to the pasta - they thaw as the pasta is cooling and as a bonus, cool the pasta faster. Makes a great main course salad. You can use any kind of pasta if you don't have farfalle.

1. Cook pasta and drain. Rinse with cold water. Put in a large bowl. Add salmon, frozen peas, and green onions to the pasta.
2. In a small bowl, combine the mayonnaise, yogurt, and dill. Pour over the pasta mixture and toss gently to combine. Chill for at least 30 minutes before serving.

Pineapple Carrot Jellied Salad

1 can	(20 oz.) crushed pineapple
1 package	lemon jelly powder
½ cup	sugar
¼ teaspoon	salt
2 tablespoons	lemon juice
1 cup	finely grated carrots
1 cup	whipping cream

Jellied salads were at the height of their popularity in the '50s and '60s. We always had to have this jellied salad for Christmas dinner.

1. Drain pineapple, reserving juice. Set pineapple aside. Mix pineapple juice with enough water to make 1 1/2 cups of liquid. Heat to a boil. Stir in jelly powder, until it is dissolved. Stir in the sugar, salt and lemon juice. Chill until it is slightly thickened.
2. Add the reserved pineapple, and the carrots. Whip the cream until stiff, and fold in to the jelly mixture. Pour into a jelly mold and chill overnight. Unmold and serve.

Vegetables

Baked Beans

3 cups	dry navy beans
4 quarts	cold water, divided
1	medium onion, chopped
1 cup	ketchup
½ cup	brown sugar
¾ cup	light molasses
2 teaspoons	salt
2 teaspoons	dry mustard
¼ pound	bacon, chopped and browned

Homemade baked beans are a delicious treat for a picnic or potluck dinner. They're good any time - make a batch for dinner and freeze the leftovers in serving size portions for future meals.

1. Rinse beans. Place in a large kettle or Dutch oven with 2 quarts water. Bring to a boil, reduce heat and simmer for 3 minutes. Remove from heat and let stand for 1 hour. Drain and rinse. Return beans to the pot and cover with remaining 2 quarts water. Bring to a boil, reduce heat and simmer for 1 hour. Drain, reserving cooking liquid.

2. In the Dutch oven or 3 quart baking dish, combine beans, 1 cup of the cooking liquid, and the remaining ingredients. Mix well. Cover and bake at 300° F. for 2 to 2 1/2 hours, or until beans are as thick as desired. Stir occasionally and add more of the reserved cooking liquid if beans seem dry after stirring. Makes 16 servings.

Apple Rutabaga Casserole

2	medium-large rutabagas
3	apples
½ cup	butter
	Salt and pepper

Turnip, or rutabaga, was a "back home" favourite. This simple, tasty recipe is great for everyday or for special occasions. Can be prepared the day before and refrigerated. Bring to room temperature and bake for 35 minutes.

1. Peel rutabagas and cut into small pieces. Place in a large saucepan of boiling water and cook until tender. Peel, core and chop apples. Add to boiling water about 5 minutes before done. Remove from heat and drain.

2. Put in food processor and mash. Add butter, salt and pepper. Spoon into casserole dish. Bake, uncovered, at 325° F. for 20 to 25 minutes.

Salads & Side Dishes - Vegetables

Sweet Potato Casserole

2	large sweet potatoes (2 lbs.)
3	eggs, beaten
¼ cup	melted butter
⅔ cup	evaporated milk or cream

TOPPING:

¾ cup	coarsely chopped pecans
½ cup	brown sugar
¼ cup	flour
2 tablespoons	melted butter

We never had sweet potatoes when we were kids, unfortunately. This recipe could be prepared the day before and refrigerated instead of baking. Bake it before dinner, increasing the baking time.

1. Peel and cut up the sweet potatoes. Boil for about 25 minutes, until tender. Drain well and mash. Stir in eggs, butter and evaporated milk. Spoon into a 2 quart baking dish.

2. Combine the topping ingredients, and sprinkle evenly over the sweet potatoes. Bake at 350° F for 40 minutes, until centre is set.

Garlic Mashed Potatoes

1 head	garlic
2 pounds	potatoes (about 5)
3 tablespoons	butter
½ cup	hot milk
	Salt and pepper

Yes, the recipe calls for a whole head of garlic, not just a clove of garlic. Baking makes it sweet and mild, and it adds great flavour to "plain old" mashed potatoes.

1. Trim 1/2 inch off the top of the garlic head. Wrap with tinfoil. Bake at 400° F. for 45 minutes.

2. Peel, cut up, and boil potatoes. Drain. Return potatoes to saucepan, and heat over low heat for 2 minutes, shaking pan occasionally, to dry them. Remove from heat.

3. Squeeze garlic out of skins into the potatoes. Add butter. Mash with potato masher until smooth. Add hot milk, salt and pepper. Stir in. Makes 4 servings.

Oven Roasted Potatoes

2 pounds	baking potatoes (about 4 potatoes)
2 tablespoons	olive oil or melted butter
2 teaspoons	paprika
½ teaspoon	salt
¼ teaspoon	pepper

You can't beat potatoes roasted in the pan with roast beef. If you are not having roast beef, these are the next best thing. This is a basic recipe which you can vary by using other herbs or spices in place of the paprika (try seasoned salt for spicy fries, or 1 teaspoon of rosemary or Italian seasoning.)

1. Peel potatoes and cut into large chunks, wedges or fries. Toss with oil, paprika, salt and pepper. Spread out in a single layer on a greased baking sheet. Bake at 400° F. for 45 to 60 minutes, until golden and tender. Makes 4 servings.

Creamy Mashed Potatoes

6	potatoes (about 2 ½ lbs.)
1 package	(4 oz.) cream cheese, softened
½ cup	sour cream
2 tablespoons	butter
1 teaspoon	onion salt
1 teaspoon	garlic salt
	Pepper
	Additional butter
	Paprika

A good special occasion potato dish. You can prepare it the day before, refrigerate, and then cook it before dinner.

1. Peel and boil potatoes until tender. Drain and mash. Add cream cheese, sour cream, butter and seasonings. Beat until fluffy and smooth. Place mixture in a casserole dish. Dot the top with butter, and sprinkle with paprika. Cover and heat at 350° F. until heated through.

Scalloped Potatoes

4 cups	thinly sliced potatoes
½ cup	thinly sliced onions
1 can	(10 oz.) cream of mushroom soup
½ cup	milk
	Salt and pepper
	Paprika

This is a very easy way to make scalloped potatoes. The soup makes them very tasty too. You can double this recipe.

1. Layer potatoes and onions in a 1 1/2 quart casserole. Mix soup, milk, and salt and pepper. Pour over top the potatoes. Sprinkle with paprika. Cover and bake at 375° F. for about 1 hour to 1 hour 15 minutes, until potatoes are cooked. Remove cover for the last 10 minutes. Makes 4 servings.

Scalloped Potatoes with Cheese

¼ cup	butter
¼ cup	flour
1½ cups	milk
1 cup	grated Cheddar cheese
6	medium potatoes, peeled and sliced
1 - 2	onions, chopped

The combination of potatoes and onions with cheese sauce makes for very tasty scalloped potatoes.

1. In a saucepan, melt butter, stir in flour and allow mixture to bubble for about 1 minute. Add milk all at once and heat to boiling, stirring constantly until thickened. Add cheese and stir until melted.

2. In a greased 8 cup casserole, layer potato and onion with sauce. Cover and bake at 350° F. for 1 hour. Uncover and bake for 10 to 20 minutes more, until potatoes are tender. Makes 6 servings.

Breads

Yorkshire Pudding

About ½ cup	beef drippings
1 cup	flour
½ teaspoon	salt
1 cup	milk
2 or 3	eggs

A British classic to serve with roast beef, one of my Grandma's Sunday dinner specialties.

1. Preheat oven to 425° F. Divide beef drippings between 8 muffin cups. Put in oven to heat. (You can use oil in place of drippings if you are making these without a roast - about 1 teaspoon per muffin cup).

2. Mix flour and salt. Add milk gradually to prevent lumping. Beat eggs well and add to batter. Remove muffin pan from the oven. Divide batter between muffin cups. Place pan back in oven. Reduce heat to 375° F. and bake until puffy and golden.

Old Fashioned Bread Stuffing

8 - 10 cups	stale bread cubes
½ cup	butter
1 cup	chopped onion
½ cup	chopped celery, with leaves
1 teaspoon	salt
¼ teaspoon	pepper
2 teaspoons	poultry seasoning (or any mixture of sage, savory, thyme, marjoram, etc.)
	Hot broth or water

I think that stuffing is one of the best parts of a turkey dinner. I never saw Mom or Grandma using a recipe to make stuffing, but here is a basic recipe to start from.

1. For a soft moist dressing, use fresh or slightly stale bread. For a lighter fluffier dressing, use quite stale or dried bread.

2. Melt butter in a frying pan. Add onion and celery, and cook until softened but not browned.

3. Combine butter mixture with bread and seasonings. If desired add some broth or water for a moister dressing. Stuff the turkey, and roast. Makes enough for an 8 to 10 pound turkey.

Buttermilk Biscuits

1 cup	buttermilk
½ cup	water
4 cups	flour
2 teaspoons	baking powder
1 teaspoon	salt
1 package	quick rising yeast
2 tablespoons	sugar
⅓ cup	shortening
2 tablespoons	melted butter

These biscuits are excellent - the addition of yeast makes them much lighter than a regular baking powder biscuit.

1. Heat buttermilk in a small pan on the stove, or in the microwave, until bubbles form around the edge. The buttermilk will curdle. Remove from heat and add water, set aside.

2. In food processor, combine flour, baking powder, salt, yeast, and sugar. Add shortening and whirl until mixture resembles coarse meal. Add buttermilk and whirl to mix in.

3. Knead the dough until smooth - if you have a large food processor you can knead in it, otherwise remove and knead about 5 minutes on a floured board. On a floured board, roll out the dough to about 3/4 inch thickness. Use a floured cookie cutter (2 1/2 to 3 inch round) to cut out the biscuits. Place on greased cookie sheets, 1 inch apart. Prick tops of biscuits with a fork.

4. Cover biscuits with a cloth and let sit for 30 to 45 minutes. They don't rise too much at this point, but will rise more during baking. Preheat oven to 400° F. Brush the biscuits with melted butter and bake for 10 to 12 minutes until lightly browned. Serve warm

Cakes, Pastries & Desserts

Cakes

Carrot Cake

CAKE:

1 cup	sugar
1 cup	cooking oil
4	eggs
1 cup	flour
1 cup	whole wheat flour
1½ teaspoons	baking soda
1 teaspoon	salt
2 teaspoons	cinnamon
2 cups	grated raw carrot
1½ cups	grated apple
1 cup	golden raisins
½ cup	chopped walnuts (optional)

CREAM CHEESE ICING:

1 package	(4 oz.) cream cheese, softened
¼ cup	butter
1 cup	icing (confectioners') sugar
½ teaspoon	vanilla

Carrot cake is always a popular standby, moist and tasty. And you can feel good about eating cake, because after all it's made from carrots! This one has apple and whole wheat flour too - even better. A food processor simplifies the preparation, making short order of grating the carrots and apples.

1. CAKE: Blend together sugar, oil and eggs. Beat until slightly thickened.

2. Mix flours, baking soda, salt and cinnamon. Combine with egg mixture. Stir in carrot, apple, raisins and nuts. Pour batter into a greased and floured 9 x 13 inch cake pan. Bake at 350° F. for 35 to 40 minutes. Remove from oven. Cool.

3. CREAM CHEESE ICING: Combine cream cheese and butter in mixer bowl. Beat on medium speed until creamy. Add icing sugar and beat until smooth. Stir in vanilla. Frost cake.

Mabel's Date Cake

CAKE:

1 cup	dates, chopped
1½ cups	boiling water
1 teaspoon	baking soda
2	eggs
1 cup	white sugar
½ cup	melted shortening or butter
1½ cups	flour
1 teaspoon	baking powder

TOPPING:

½ cup	brown sugar
½ cup	chopped walnuts
1 package	(6 oz.) butterscotch chips

This recipe is from my (late) Great Aunt Mabel, who gave the recipe to my Mom, who gave the recipe to me.

1. CAKE: Start this cake the night before: combine dates, boiling water and baking soda. Cool and leave to soak overnight.

2. The next day: beat eggs, sugar and shortening together. Stir in flour and baking powder. Mix until smooth. Add dates. Pour batter into a greased 9 x 13 inch cake pan.

3. TOPPING: Sprinkle brown sugar evenly over top of the cake. Sprinkle butterscotch chips over, then walnuts. Bake at 350° F. for 40 minutes.

The Best Chocolate Cake

CAKE:

3 squares	(1 oz. each) unsweetened chocolate
½ cup	butter
2¼ cups	light brown sugar
3	eggs
1½ teaspoons	vanilla
2 cups	flour
2 teaspoons	baking soda
½ teaspoon	salt
1 cup	sour cream
1 cup	boiling water

7 MINUTE FROSTING:

2	egg whites
1½ cups	white or brown sugar
¼ cup	cold water
2 tablespoons	corn syrup
¼ teaspoon	salt
1 teaspoon	vanilla

This chocolate cake always gets rave reviews. Ice with 7 Minute Frosting, or use the filling and frosting of your choice. The cake can also be baked in a 9 x 13 inch cake pan - increase the baking time to 45 to 50 minutes.

7 Minute Frosting is a tasty light fluffy frosting. Don't try to make it on a humid day - it will turn out grainy instead of fluffy.

1. CAKE: Melt chocolate, either on the stove or in the microwave. Set aside.

2. Beat butter in large mixer bowl. Add brown sugar and eggs, and beat until light and fluffy, about 5 minutes. Add vanilla and melted chocolate, and beat to combine.

3. Combine flour, baking soda, and salt. Add to chocolate mixture gradually, alternating with sour cream. Beat after each addition. Stir boiling water into the batter - the batter will be thin.

4. Pour into two 9 inch round cake pans which have been greased and floured. Bake at 350° F. for 35 minutes, until cake centre springs back when touched. Cool for 10 minutes. Remove from pans and cool completely.

5. 7 MINUTE FROSTING: In top of double boiler, combine egg whites, sugar, water, corn syrup and salt. Cook over boiling water, beating with hand or rotary mixer, until it will stand in peaks, about 7 minutes. Remove from heat, beat in vanilla. Fill and frost cooled cake.

Cocoa Cake

CAKE:

⅓ cup	butter
¾ cup	sugar
1	egg
1 cup	flour
⅓ cup	cocoa
½ teaspoon	baking soda
⅛ teaspoon	baking powder
½ teaspoon	salt
⅔ cup	water
½ teaspoon	vanilla

CREAMY NUT ICING:

¼ cup	butter
4 teaspoons	flour
Pinch	salt
¼ cup	milk
1½ cups	icing (confectioners') sugar
¾ teaspoon	vanilla
¼ cup	chopped walnuts

An easy way to satisfy a chocolate cake craving. This creamy icing is great with it, but you could also use a chocolate icing or whatever you prefer.

1. CAKE: In mixer bowl, beat butter, sugar and egg together until light and fluffy.

2. Mix flour, cocoa, baking soda, baking powder and salt together. Mix water and vanilla together.

3. Remove beaters and add flour mixture to egg mixture alternately with water. Fold until smooth. Spread batter in a greased 8 inch square pan. Bake at 350° F. for 30 minutes, until top of cake springs back when touched lightly. Remove from oven and cool.

4. CREAMY NUT ICING: Melt butter. Sprinkle in flour and salt. Stir to blend. Remove from heat. Stir in milk, all at once. Return to moderate heat and cook, stirring constantly, until thick and smooth (don't worry if it separates a little).

5. Remove from heat and stir in icing sugar and vanilla. Set in a pan of ice water and stir until the frosting is thick enough to spread. Stir in nuts. Spread over top of the cooled cake.

Sour Cream Cake

CAKE:

1	egg
1 cup	brown sugar
1 cup	sour cream
¾ cup	flaked coconut
2 cups	flour
1 teaspoon	baking soda
1 teaspoon	salt

CARAMEL ICING:

1 cup	brown sugar
⅓ cup	butter
⅓ cup	milk
1 cup	icing (confectioners') sugar

This cake is a little different, and very easy with only a few ingredients. The caramel icing is delicious, and also goes great with chocolate cake.

1. CAKE: Beat egg. Gradually add sugar and continue to beat until light. Stir in sour cream and coconut.

2. In small bowl combine flour, baking soda and salt. Add to egg mixture and beat well. Spread batter in a greased 9 inch square pan. Bake at 375° F. for 25 minutes, until top of cake springs back when touched lightly. Cool.

3. CARAMEL ICING: Combine brown sugar, butter and milk in a small saucepan. Bring to a boil. Continue to boil, stirring constantly, for 3 minutes. Cool to lukewarm.

4. Stir in icing sugar and continue to stir until the right consistency to spread. Spread over cooled cake.

Banana Cream Cake

CAKE:

2⅔ cups	flour
1 tablespoon	baking powder
½ teaspoon	baking soda
¾ teaspoon	salt
¼ teaspoon	nutmeg
3	eggs
¾ cup	light brown sugar
2 teaspoons	vanilla
1 cup	mashed banana (about 3 medium)
1 cup	whipping cream
¾ cup	finely chopped pecans

CREAM CHEESE ICING:

2 packages	(8 oz. each) cream cheese, softened
¼ cup	butter
1½ to 2 cups	icing (confectioners') sugar
1 teaspoon	vanilla

A great special occasion layer cake. You can decorate the cake with pecans if you like.

1. CAKE: In a small bowl, combine flour, baking powder, baking soda, salt and nutmeg.

2. In large bowl of electric mixer, beat eggs well at medium speed. Gradually add brown sugar and continue to beat until mixture is thick and light. Stir in vanilla and bananas.

3. In a small bowl, whip the cream. Beat half of the flour mixture into the eggs. Continue beating at low speed until blended. Add whipped cream and then remaining flour mixture. Fold in pecans.

4. Divide batter between 2 greased 8 inch round cake pans. Bake at 350° F. for 35 minutes, until cake tests done. Remove from oven. Cool 10 minutes in pans, remove from pans and cool completely.

5. CREAM CHEESE ICING: Combine cream cheese and butter in mixer bowl. Beat on medium speed until creamy. Add icing sugar and beat until smooth. Stir in vanilla. Fill and frost cake.

Pat's Boiled Raisin Cake

CAKE:

2 cups	raisins
3 cups	water
2 cups	flour
1 teaspoon	baking soda
1 teaspoon	cinnamon
1 teaspoon	cloves
1 teaspoon	nutmeg
½ cup	butter
1 cup	white sugar
2	eggs
1 teaspoon	vanilla

CARAMEL ICING:

¼ cup	butter
½ cup	brown sugar
2 tablespoons	whole milk or cream
1 cup	icing (confectioners') sugar
1 teaspoon	vanilla

This was my Mom's famous cake, which she made for many, many occasions. And we also used to have it at home for no occasion at all!

1. CAKE: Boil raisins and water until there is one cup of juice remaining. Remove from heat and cool.

2. In a small bowl, combine flour, baking soda and spices.

3. In mixer bowl, cream together butter and sugar. Beat in eggs. Stir in vanilla.

4. Drain raisins and reserve juice. Add raisins to the creamed mixture. Add flour mixture and stir to combine. Add reserved raisin juice (1 cup) last. Spread batter in a greased 11 x 7 inch oblong or 9 inch square pan. Bake at 350° F. for 35 to 40 minutes, until top of cake springs back when touched lightly. Cool.

5. CARAMEL ICING: Melt butter. Add brown sugar. Stir over low heat for 2 minutes. Add milk and stir until it comes to a boil. Remove from heat and add icing sugar. Beat until creamy. Stir in vanilla. Spread over top of cooled cake.

Lazy Daisy Oatmeal Cake

CAKE:

1 cup	uncooked rolled oats (instant or regular)
1¼ cups	boiling water
½ cup	butter
1 cup	white sugar
1 cup	brown sugar
2	eggs
1 teaspoon	vanilla
1½ cups	flour
1½ teaspoons	baking soda
½ teaspoon	salt
¾ teaspoon	cinnamon
¼ teaspoon	nutmeg

TOPPING:

¼ cup	butter, melted
½ cup	brown sugar
3 tablespoons	cream or milk
¾ cup	flaked coconut
⅓ cup	chopped nuts

I don't know why this cake is called lazy daisy, but it is good.

1. CAKE: In a shallow bowl, combine rolled oats and boiling water. Let sit for 20 minutes.

2. In mixer bowl cream butter. Add sugars and beat until light. Beat in eggs and vanilla.

3. In another bowl, mix flour, baking soda, salt and spices. Remove beaters from creamed mixture. Stir in rolled oat mixture. Fold in flour mixture. Pour batter into a greased 9 inch square cake pan. Bake at 350° F. for 40 to 50 minutes. Remove from oven.

4. TOPPING: Combine all ingredients. Spread over the hot cake. Return the cake to the oven, under the broiler. Broil until the topping is bubbly and tinged with gold. Watch it as it will burn easily.

Hot Milk Cake

CAKE:
1 tablespoon	butter
½ cup	milk
2	eggs
1 cup	white sugar
1 teaspoon	vanilla
1 cup	flour
½ teaspoon	salt
1 teaspoon	baking powder

TOPPING:
5 tablespoons	butter
5 tablespoons	brown or white sugar
3 tablespoons	milk or cream
¾ cup	coconut

This is good when it is still warm (and when it is cooled too.) The cake is a light cake that you can also use without the topping. It makes a nice base for strawberry shortcake (top slices with sweetened strawberries and whipped cream) or with fruit and ice cream, etc.

1. CAKE: Heat milk and butter together until milk is hot but not boiling, and butter is melted.

2. In mixer bowl, beat eggs and sugar together until very light. Stir in vanilla.

3. Mix flour, salt and baking powder together. Remove beaters and add flour mixture to egg mixture alternately with milk-butter mixture. Fold until smooth. Spread batter in a greased 9 inch square pan. Bake at 350° F. for 20 minutes, until top of cake springs back when touched lightly.

4. TOPPING: Melt butter. Add sugar, milk and coconut. Carefully spread topping over hot cake. Place under hot broiler and watch until bubbly and golden.

Apple Coffee Cake

About 5	apples
3 teaspoons	cinnamon
⅓ cup	sugar (1st amount)
4½ cups	flour
4 teaspoons	baking powder
3 cups	sugar (2nd amount)
1 teaspoon	salt
6	large eggs
1½ cups	good quality oil
⅓ cup	frozen orange juice concentrate, undiluted

We used to have this cake frequently at home when we were kids. It was my brother Bob's favourite. It can be served warm on it's own, or with ice cream or whipped cream.

1. Prepare apples first: wash, pare, core and dice. Measure 4 cups. To them add cinnamon and 1/3 cup sugar. Mix well and set aside while you make the batter.

2. In a large bowl, mix the flour, baking powder, remaining sugar and salt. Add eggs, oil and orange juice concentrate. Beat until smooth and blended.

3. Grease a 10 inch tube pan. Spoon 1/3 of the batter into the pan. Thoroughly drain any juice from the apples. Spoon 1/2 of the apples over the batter. Top with another 1/3 of the batter, then the remaining apples. Top with the remaining cake batter. Bake at 325° F. for 1 1/2 hours. Be sure not to underbake.

Buttermilk Chocolate Cake

CAKE:

2 cups	flour
2 cups	sugar
½ cup	butter
¼ cup	cocoa
1 cup	cold water
½ cup	buttermilk
1 teaspoon	vanilla
1 teaspoon	cinnamon
¼ teaspoon	salt
1 teaspoon	baking soda
2	eggs, beaten

ICING:

½ cup	butter
¼ cup	cocoa
5 tablespoons	buttermilk
4 cups	icing (confectioners') sugar
1 teaspoon	vanilla

This recipe is from Auntie Bess who has been baking it since my four cousins were small. She says they were forever offering at school "my Mom will make a cake," and most often this would be the cake she would make!

1. CAKE: In a large bowl combine the flour and sugar.

2. In a small saucepan, or in a microwave dish, combine the butter, cocoa and water. Heat to boiling. Pour over the flour mixture and mix well.

3. Add buttermilk, vanilla, cinnamon, salt, baking soda and eggs. Mix well. Pour batter into a greased jelly roll pan. Bake at 400° F. for 20 minutes.

4. ICING: 5 minutes before the cake is done, combine butter, cocoa and buttermilk in a medium saucepan. Bring to a boil. Remove from heat, beat in icing sugar and vanilla. Beat until smooth. Remove cake from oven and spread icing while the cake is hot.

Chocolate Caramel Pecan Cake

FILLING:

1 package	(14 oz.) caramels (about 75)
1 can	sweetened condensed milk
½ cup	butter

CAKE:

⅔ cup	butter
4 squares	(1 oz. each) unsweetened chocolate
1½ cups	water
2 cups	sugar
2	eggs
2½ cups	flour
1 teaspoon	salt
1 teaspoon	baking soda
2 teaspoons	vanilla
1½ cups	coarsely chopped pecans

Mmmm, I love Turtles! This cake is kind of an upside down Turtles cake (since the pecans are on the top). A great special occasion cake, topped off with a scoop of caramel ice cream.

1. FILLING: Unwrap caramels and combine in a saucepan with sweetened condensed milk and butter. Cook and stir over medium heat until melted and smooth. Remove from heat and set aside.

2. CAKE: Melt butter and chocolate together, either on the stove or in the microwave. Add the water, sugar, eggs, flour, salt, baking soda and vanilla. Beat until smooth and creamy. Spread half of the cake batter into a greased 9 x 13 inch pan. Bake at 350° F. for 15 minutes, until the centre is set. Remove from oven.

3. Spread filling evenly over the cake. Spread the remaining cake batter over the filling. Sprinkle the nuts over the top. Return to the oven and bake 40 minutes, until cake springs back when touched. Cool completely before cutting.

Yule Log

CAKE:

⅔ cup	flour
¼ teaspoon	soda
¼ teaspoon	salt
4	eggs
¾ cup	sugar
3 squares	(1 oz. each) unsweetened chocolate
2 tablespoons	water

FILLING:

1 cup	whipping cream
1 teaspoon	vanilla
2 tablespoons	icing (confectioners') sugar

ICING:

⅓ cup	butter
2 cups	icing (confectioners') sugar
¼ cup	cocoa
2 tablespoons	milk
½ teaspoon	vanilla

I would always make this Yule Log for New Year's Day dinner. The recipe is long, but it's easy to make and looks very impressive. It tastes good too!

1. CAKE: Grease a 15 x 10 inch jelly roll pan, and line with waxed paper. Grease waxed paper. Mix flour, soda and salt together.

2. Beat eggs in a small mixer bowl at high speed, until thick and light - about 5 minutes. Gradually add the sugar, and beat until thick.

3. Melt the chocolate and water together, and add to the egg mixture. Fold in the dry ingredients, and mix gently but thoroughly.

4. Spread in prepared pan, and bake at 350° F. for 15 to 17 minutes, until the cake springs back when lightly touched.

5. Remove from oven and turn out immediately onto a tea towel that has been sprinkled generously with icing sugar. Remove waxed paper, and trim off any crisp edges of the cake. Begin at the narrow end, and roll up the cake and the tea towel together. Allow to cool.

Yule Log - continued

6. FILLING: Whip cream until soft peaks form. Stir in vanilla and icing sugar and whip until stiff. Unroll the cake when cool, and spread the top with the whip cream. Re-roll, without the towel. Cut a thin slice off of each end of the roll, to make them even.

7. ICING: Soften butter. Combine all ingredients and beat until smooth and of good spreading consistency. Use the centres of the ends you sliced off the cake to make "bumps on the log": use a little of the icing to affix the bump to the side of the cake - one on each side.

8. Ice the entire cake with the icing, including the ends and the bumps. Run a fork along the icing so that it resembles tree bark. Sprinkle with icing sugar (snow), and decorate with holly or other Christmas decoration leaves. Store in refrigerator.

Graham Wafer Cake

2 tablespoons	butter
1 cup	sugar
1	egg, beaten
2 tablespoons	flour
1½ teaspoons	baking powder
1½ cups	graham wafer crumbs
1 cup	whole milk

This recipe is from my Auntie Bess. If you like graham wafers you will enjoy this tasty cake.

1. In mixer bowl, cream together butter and sugar. Beat in egg.

2. Combine flour, baking powder and graham wafer crumbs. Remove beaters. Add the dry ingredients, alternately with milk. Spread batter in a greased 8 inch square pan. Bake at 350° F. for 30 minutes, until top of cake springs back when touched lightly. Cool. Ice with lemon butter icing.

Pies

Never-Fail Pastry

5½ cups	flour
2 teaspoons	salt
1 pound	lard or shortening
1	egg
1 tablespoon	vinegar
	Cold water

The trickiest part about making a pie is the crust. Try this never-fail pastry recipe for a nice flaky pie crust.

1. In a large bowl mix the flour and salt. Cut in lard or shortening until mixture resembles coarse meal.

2. In a measuring cup, beat together egg and vinegar. Add enough cold water to make 1 cup of liquid. Add liquid to flour mixture a little at a time, while stirring with a fork. Add just enough liquid to make the dough hold together. Press into a ball.

3. Pastry can be used right away, or stored in fridge for up to 2 weeks or in the freezer for up to 3 months (separate dough into 6 balls.) Bring pastry to room temperature before rolling out. Makes enough for 6 single crust or 3 double crust pies.

Apple Pie

	Pastry for a 2 crust 9" pie
5 cups	peeled and thinly sliced apples (about 5 - 7 apples)
¾ to 1 cup	sugar
1 teaspoon	cinnamon
1 tablespoon	butter

"Apple pie without the cheese, is like a kiss without the squeeze." Needless to say, we enjoyed our apple pie with a slice of Cheddar cheese. It's also good with a scoop of ice cream.

1. Combine sliced apples, sugar and cinnamon in bowl. (Amount of sugar depends on tartness of apples.)

2. Roll out half the pastry and line a 9 inch pie plate. Fill with apple mixture. Dot with butter.

3. Fit top pastry over apples. Make slits for escape of steam. Seal edges and flute a high edge. Bake at 425° F. for 25 to 30 minutes until apples are tender.

Apple Crisp Pie

Pastry for a deep 9" pie

Like apple crisp, but in a pie.

FILLING:

4 cups	peeled and sliced tart apples
½ cup	white sugar
½ teaspoon	nutmeg
2 teaspoons	lemon juice
¼ cup	raisins (optional)

TOPPING:

¾ cup	flour
½ cup	light brown sugar
½ teaspoon	salt
⅓ cup	butter

1. FILLING: In a bowl, mix the sliced apples with the sugar, nutmeg, lemon juice and raisins (if used).

2. Roll out the pastry to fit a 9 inch deep dish pie plate. With thumb and finger, shape a high fluted edge. Fill with apple mixture.

3. TOPPING: Combine flour, brown sugar and salt. Cut in butter until the size of peas. Sprinkle over apples and pat down. Bake at 425° F. for 10 minutes. Reduce heat to 325° and bake for 35 to 40 minutes longer, until apples are tender and topping is rich gold.

Pumpkin Pie

	Pastry for a 1 crust 9" pie
2	eggs, slightly beaten
1¾ cups	canned or cooked pumpkin
¾ cup	sugar
½ teaspoon	salt
1 teaspoon	cinnamon
½ teaspoon	ginger
¼ teaspoon	cloves
1⅔ cups	evaporated milk

The classic pumpkin pie is a must-have for Thanksgiving dinner, served topped with whipped cream. It is extra special made with fresh pumpkin.

1. Roll out pastry and line a 9 inch pie plate. Mix all remaining ingredients in a large bowl. Pour into pastry shell. Bake at 425° F. for 15 minutes. Reduce temperature to 350° F and continue baking for 45 minutes, or until knife inserted in centre comes out clean.

Rhubarb Strawberry Pie

	Pastry for a 2 crust 9" pie
4 cups	chopped rhubarb, fresh or frozen
2 cups	sliced strawberries
1⅓ cups	white sugar
¼ cup	cornstarch
1 tablespoon	lemon juice
¼ teaspoon	cinnamon
1	egg, beaten

The classic springtime dessert - delicious. Especially with a scoop of vanilla ice cream!

1. Roll out half the pastry and line a 9 inch pie plate. Trim leaving 1/2 inch over the pie plate. Combine rhubarb, strawberries, sugar, cornstarch, lemon juice and cinnamon. Place in the pie shell.

2. Roll out remaining pastry and cut into 1 inch strips. Make a lattice top crust on the pie by crisscrossing the strips over the filling. Trim the strips even with the pie plate. Fold the 1/2 inch of the bottom crust over the ends of the strips. Seal and flute the edges. Brush lattice with egg.

3. Place on a baking sheet or tinfoil in the oven and bake at 425° F. for 15 minutes, until the crust starts to brown. Reduce heat to 375° and continue to bake for 50 to 60 minutes, until crust is golden, rhubarb is tender, and filling is thickened.

Sour Cream Rhubarb Crumb Pie

	Pastry for a 1 crust 10" pie
4 cups	cubed rhubarb
1½ cups	white sugar
⅓ cup	flour
1 cup	sour cream

TOPPING:

½ cup	flour
½ cup	brown sugar
¼ cup	soft butter

This was my Mom's favourite rhubarb dessert, which I used to make for her (and the rest of us) when I lived at home - she wasn't much for making pies.

1. Roll out the pie crust and line a 10 inch pie plate or 9 inch deep dish pie plate. Trim even with the edge of the pie plate. Arrange rhubarb in the pie shell. Mix together the sugar, flour and sour cream. Pour mixture over the rhubarb.

2. TOPPING: In a small bowl combine the flour and brown sugar. Stir in the butter until crumbly. Sprinkle over the rhubarb. Bake at 450° F. for 15 minutes. Reduce heat to 350° and continue to bake for another 30 minutes.

Rhubarb Crumble Pie

Pastry for a 1 crust 9" pie

If you like rhubarb crisp, you will like this recipe from Auntie Bess.

FILLING:
5 cups	chopped rhubarb
¼ cup	water
¾ cup	sugar
3 tablespoons	flour

TOPPING:
1 tablespoon	butter
2 tablespoons	sugar
2 tablespoons	flour
2 tablespoons	rolled oats

HONEY LEMON YOGURT SAUCE:
1¼ cups	vanilla yogurt
3 tablespoons	liquid honey
¾ teaspoon	grated lemon rind

1. FILLING: In large saucepan place rhubarb and water.
2. Stir together sugar and flour; add to rhubarb. Cook over medium heat until boiling. Reduce heat and simmer, partially covered until rhubarb is tender (about 5 minutes, don't let it get mushy). Set aside.
3. TOPPING: Combine butter, sugar, flour and oats for topping. Blend until mixture resembles coarse crumbs.
4. Spread filling in pastry shell, cover with topping. Bake 35 to 40 minutes in 350° F. oven. Serve warm or cool with Honey Lemon Yogurt Sauce.
5. HONEY LEMON YOGURT SAUCE: In small bowl stir together yogurt, liquid honey and lemon rind. Refrigerate until serving time.

Flapper Pie

CRUST:
1¼ cups	graham wafer crumbs
¼ cup	sugar
½ teaspoon	cinnamon
¼ cup	melted butter

FILLING:
½ cup	sugar
3 tablespoons	cornstarch
2 cups	milk
2	egg yolks, lightly beaten
1 teaspoon	vanilla

MERINGUE:
2	egg whites
3 tablespoons	icing (confectioners') sugar

This cream pie with a meringue topping is an old time prairie classic.

1. CRUST: Combine crumbs, sugar and cinnamon. Blend in butter until moistened. Reserve 1/4 cup of mixture. Press remainder onto bottom and sides of a 9 inch pie plate. Bake at 375° F. for 8 minutes. Cool.

2. FILLING: In saucepan, blend sugar and cornstarch. Blend in milk. Cook and stir over medium heat until boiling.

3. Stir a little hot milk mixture into egg yolks. Stir egg yolks into pan. Cook and stir over low heat until thickened, about 2 minutes. Remove from heat and add vanilla. Cool slightly and pour into crust.

4. MERINGUE: Beat egg whites until soft peaks form. Gradually beat in sugar until stiff peaks form. Spread over filling and seal to crust. Top with the reserved crumbs. Bake at 400° F. for 5 minutes, until lightly browned. Cool completely before serving.

Cheesecakes

Marble Chocolate Cheesecake

CRUST:
1¼ cups	chocolate wafer crumb
¼ cup	melted butter s

FILLING:
2 packages	(8 oz. each) cream cheese, softened
1 cup	sugar
2	eggs
1 teaspoon	vanilla
1 tablespoon	grated lemon rind
¼ cup	lemon juice
2 cups	sour cream
4 squares	(1 oz. each) semi-sweet chocolate, melted

This is an outstanding looking cheesecake - and it tastes just as good as it looks!

1. CRUST: Combine chocolate wafer crumbs and melted butter. Press into the bottom of a 9 inch springform pan.

2. FILLING: In a large mixer bowl, beat cream cheese with sugar until light. Add eggs one at a time, while beating. Stir in vanilla.

3. Take 3 cups of this mixture and add lemon rind, juice, and 1 1/2 cups of the sour cream. Pour over crust.

4. To the remaining cheesecake mixture add the remaining sour cream and the melted chocolate.

5. Spoon the chocolate mixture over top of the lemon cheesecake mixture. Cut through it with the end of a knife to create a swirled marble effect.

6. Bake at 350° F. for 45 to 60 minutes. The sides should have risen but the centre will still be wobbly. Turn off the oven and leave the cheesecake in it for another 30 minutes. Remove and let cool completely. Refrigerate at least 3 to 4 hours before serving.

Unbaked Cherry Cheesecake

CRUST:
⅓ cup	butter, melted
1¼ cups	graham wafer crumbs
¼ cup	sugar

FILLING:
1 package	(8 oz.) cream cheese, softened
1 can	sweetened condensed milk
⅓ cup	lemon juice
1 teaspoon	vanilla
1 can	cherry pie filling

I started making this when I was a kid - the recipe is from the back of the Eagle Brand milk can. You can use other pie or fruit toppings as desired.

1. CRUST: Combine butter, graham wafer crumbs and sugar. Press into a 9 inch pie plate.
2. FILLING: In a medium mixer bowl, beat cream cheese until light and fluffy. Gradually stir in sweetened condensed milk until thoroughly blended. Stir in lemon juice and vanilla. Pour into crust. Chill 2 to 3 hours (or overnight). Top wih cherry pie filling before serving.

Apple Cheesecake

CRUST:
½ cup	butter
⅓ cup	sugar
1 cup	flour

FILLING:
1 package	(8 oz.) cream cheese, softened
½ cup	sugar
1	egg
1 teaspoon	vanilla

TOPPING:
1½ pounds	apples
¼ cup	sugar
½ teaspoon	cinnamon
¼ cup	sliced almonds

This tasty cheesecake is easy to make and is a very attractive dessert.

1. CRUST: Cream butter and sugar. Add flour and mix well. Press into the bottom and half way up sides of a 9 inch springform pan.

2. FILLING: Mix cream cheese and sugar. Add egg and vanilla and blend well. Spoon over crust.

3. TOPPING: Core, peel and thinly slice apples. Combine sugar and cinnamon. Sprinkle over apples and toss to coat apples on both sides. Arrange apples in a pinwheel fashion over the filling. Sprinkle almonds over top. Bake at 450° F. for 10 minutes, reduce heat to 400° F. and bake for 25 minutes. Cool to room temperature (3 to 4 hours) and then refrigerate until serving.

Baileys Marble Cheesecake

CRUST:
¼ cup	butter, melted
1½ cups	chocolate wafer crumbs

FILLING:
3 packages	(8 oz. each) cream cheese, softened
¾ cup	sugar
3	eggs
2 cups	sour cream
¼ cup	Baileys Irish Cream liqueur
1 teaspoon	vanilla
6 squares	(1 oz. each) semi-sweet chocolate, melted

TOPPING:
5 squares	(1 oz. each) semi-sweet chocolate
½ cup	whipping cream
2 tablespoons	butter
½ teaspoon	vanilla

Another yummy cheesecake - very attractive too with the chocolate crust and topping and marble filling in between.

1. CRUST: Combine butter and chocolate wafer crumbs. Press into the bottom of a 10 inch springform pan. Bake for 10 minutes at 325° F.

2. FILLING: In a large mixer bowl, beat cream cheese and sugar until light and fluffy. Add eggs one at a time while beating. Stir in sour cream, Baileys, and vanilla. Pour 2/3 of the cheesecake mixture over the crust.

3. To the remaining mixture stir the melted chocolate. Spoon the chocolate mixture by large spoonfuls over the plain cheesecake mixture. Run a knife through it a few times to create a marbled effect. Bake at 325° F. for about 1 and 1/2 hours, until the centre is raised and set. Let cool to room temperature.

4. TOPPING: Coarsely chop the chocolate. Mix with whipping cream and butter and melt (on the stove or in microwave). Stir in vanilla. Spread over top of the cheesecake. Refrigerate at least 6 hours, or overnight.

Peanut Butter Chocolate Cheesecake

CRUST:

¼ cup	butter, melted
1 cup	graham wafer crumbs
¼ cup	sugar

FILLING:

12 oz.	cream cheese, softened (1-8 oz., 1-4 oz. package)
1½ cups	peanut butter
1 cup	sugar
1 cup	whipping cream

TOPPING:

½ cup	sugar
½ cup	whipping cream
1 teaspoon	vanilla
4 squares	(1 oz. each) semi-sweet chocolate
¼ cup	butter

A definite winner with all the peanut butter and chocolate lovers.

1. CRUST: Combine butter, graham wafer crumbs and sugar. Press into the bottom of a 10 inch springform pan. Bake for 10 minutes at 350° F. Cool completely before adding filling.

2. FILLING: In a large mixer bowl, beat cream cheese, peanut butter and sugar until light and fluffy. Whip cream and fold into peanut butter mixture. Pour over cooled crust.

3. TOPPING: Combine sugar, cream and vanilla in a saucepan. Stir to blend. Place over medium-high heat and bring to a boil. Reduce heat and simmer for 5 minutes - do not stir. Remove from heat and add chocolate and butter. Stir with a wooden spoon until chocolate has melted and the mixture becomes quite shiny - about 5 minutes. Pour over filling. Refrigerate at least 8 hours, or overnight.

Chocolate Turtle Cheesecake

CRUST:
2 cups	chocolate wafer crumbs
⅓ cup	melted butter

FILLING:
1 bag	(14 oz.) caramels (about 75)
⅔ cup	evaporated milk
1 cup	chopped pecans, toasted
2 packages	(8 oz. each) cream cheese, softened
½ cup	sugar
1 teaspoon	vanilla
2	eggs
½ cup	semi-sweet chocolate chips, melted

A cheesecake inspired by Turtles chocolates. If desired you can top it with chocolate curls, or chocolate sauce, or whipped cream and pecans.

1. CRUST: Combine chocolate wafer crumbs and melted butter. Press into the bottom of a 9 inch springform pan. Bake at 350° F. for 10 minutes.

2. FILLING: In a heavy saucepan, combine caramels and evaporated milk. Heat over low heat, stirring frequently, until melted and smooth. Pour over crust. Top with pecans.

3. In a large mixer bowl, beat cream cheese with sugar and vanilla until light. Add eggs one at a time, while beating. Stir in melted chocolate. Pour over pecans in crust. Bake at 350° F. for 40 minutes. Remove and let cool completely. Refrigerate at least 3 to 4 hours before serving.

Chocolate Chip Cheesecake

CRUST:
¼ cup	butter
1½ cups	Oreo cookie crumbs (about 18 cookies)

FILLING:
3 packages	(8 oz. each) cream cheese, softened
1 can	sweetened condensed milk
3	eggs
2 teaspoons	vanilla
1 cup	mini chocolate chips
1 teaspoon	flour

Who doesn't like chocolate chips? This one is sure to be a hit.

1. CRUST: Combine butter and Oreo cookie crumbs. Press into the bottom of a 9 inch springform pan.

2. FILLING: In a large mixer bowl, beat cream cheese until fluffy. Add sweetened condensed milk and beat until smooth. Add eggs and vanilla and mix well.

3. In a small bowl, combine 1/2 cup of chocolate chips with the 1 teaspoon flour. Toss to coat. Stir into the cheese mixture. Pour over crust. Sprinkle the remaining chocolate chips over top. Bake for 1 hour at 300° F., or until cake springs back when lightly touched. Cool to room temperature and then chill until serving.

Creamy Baked Cheesecake

CRUST:

⅓ cup	butter, melted
1¼ cups	graham wafer crumbs
¼ cup	sugar

FILLING:

2 packages	(8 oz. each) cream cheese, softened
1 can	sweetened condensed milk
3	eggs
¼ cup	lemon juice

A good, simple recipe for a classic cheesecake. Serve topped with your choice of fruit sauce, if desired.

1. CRUST: Combine butter, graham wafer crumbs and sugar. Press into the bottom of a 9 inch springform pan.

2. FILLING: In a large mixer bowl, beat cream cheese until fluffy. Add sweetened condensed milk and beat until smooth. Add eggs and lemon juice and mix well. Pour over crust. Bake for 50 to 55 minutes at 300° F. Cake is done when it springs back when lightly touched. Cool to room temperature and then chill until serving. Garnish as desired.

Chocolate Cheesecake

CRUST:
⅓ cup	butter, melted
1¼ cups	chocolate wafer crumbs

FILLING:
3 packages	(8 oz. each) cream cheese, softened
1 can	sweetened condensed milk
8 squares	(1 oz. each) semi-sweet chocolate, melted
4	eggs
2 teaspoons	vanilla

Sure to be popular with chocolate lovers. Make it the day before serving so it can chill overnight, and the great milk chocolate flavour can develop.

1. CRUST: Combine butter and chocolate wafer crumbs. Press into the bottom of a 9 inch springform pan.

2. FILLING: In a large mixer bowl, beat cream cheese until fluffy. Add sweetened condensed milk and beat until smooth. Add chocolate, eggs and vanilla and mix well. Pour over crust. Bake for 1 hour 5 minutes at 300° F. Cool to room temperature and then chill until serving.

S'mores Cheesecake

CRUST:

½ cup	butter, melted
2¼ cups	graham wafer crumbs
⅓ cup	sugar

FILLING:

2 packages	(8 oz. each) cream cheese, softened
1 can	sweetened condensed milk
2 teaspoons	vanilla
3	eggs
1 cup	miniature chocolate chips
1 cup	miniature marshmallow

TOPPING:

1 cup	miniature marshmallows
½ cup	chocolate chips
1 tablespoon	butter

Did you ever make s'mores around the campfire? Well then you'll like s'mores cheesecake!

1. CRUST: Combine butter, graham wafer crumbs and sugar. Press into the bottom of a 10 inch springform pan.

2. FILLING: In a large mixer bowl, beat cream cheese, sweetened condensed milk, and vanilla until smooth. Add eggs and beat until combined. Stir in chocolate chips and marshmallows. Pour over crust. Bake at 325° F. for 40 to 45 minutes, until centre is almost set.

3. TOPPING: Remove cheesecake from oven and sprinkle marshmallows over top. Return to the oven and bake another 4 to 6 minutes, until the marshmallows are puffed.

4. Melt chocolate chips and butter together. Drizzle over the marshmallows. Let cool to room temperature and then refrigerate overnight.

White Chocolate Cheesecake

CRUST:
1½ cups	vanilla wafer crumbs
⅓ cup	melted butter

FILLING:
2 packages	(8 oz. each) cream cheese, softened
½ cup	sugar
2 teaspoons	lemon juice
3	eggs
1 cup	sour cream
1 teaspoon	vanilla
8 squares	(1 oz. each) white chocolate, melted

TOPPING:
1 cup	sour cream
2 tablespoons	sugar
½ teaspoon	vanilla

For an attractive variation, you can make this with a dark chocolate crust (use chocolate wafers instead of vanilla) and dark chocolate curls on top.

1. CRUST: Combine vanilla wafer crumbs and melted butter. Press into the bottom of a 9 inch springform pan.

2. FILLING: In a large mixer bowl, beat cream cheese with sugar and lemon juice until light. Add eggs one at a time, while beating. Stir in sour cream, melted chocolate and vanilla until evenly mixed. Pour over crust. Bake at 350° F. for 40 to 45 minutes, until just set.

3. TOPPING: Mix sour cream, sugar and vanilla together. Remove cheesecake from oven and spread topping over top. Return to the oven for 5 minutes. Remove and cool. Refrigerate for at least 5 hours or overnight. Garnish with white chocolate curls, fruit, or fruit sauce if desired.

Raspberry White Chocolate Cheesecake

CRUST:
2 cups	vanilla wafer crumbs
½ cup	melted butter

FILLING:
4 packages	(8 oz. each) cream cheese, softened
½ cup	sugar
4	large eggs
2 tablespoons	flour
1½ teaspoons	vanilla
¼ teaspoon	almond extract
8 squares	(1 oz. each) white chocolate, melted
2 cups	fresh raspberries
1 tablespoon	cornstarch

This makes a very large dessert, and a very popular one. You can use frozen raspberries if fresh are not available and it will be just as good - thaw, drain and pat them dry before using.

1. CRUST: Combine wafers and butter. Press into the bottom and 2/3 up the sides of a 10 inch springform pan.

2. FILLING: In a large mixer bowl, beat cream cheese until fluffy. Beat in the sugar and add eggs one at a time. Gradually stir in flour, vanilla and almond extract. Slowly add melted chocolate and beat until combined.

3. Toss raspberries with cornstarch. Sprinkle over the crust. Pour the cheesecake mixture over top.

4. Put in oven which has been preheated to 350° F. Immediately turn the oven down to 250°. Bake for 1 3/4 to 2 hours, until cheesecake is set in the centre. Let cool and then refrigerate overnight. Garnish with additional raspberries.

Unbaked Chocolate Cheesecake

CRUST:
½ cup	butter, melted
2 cups	chocolate wafer crumbs

FILLING:
1 package	(8 oz.) cream cheese, softened
½ cup	sugar
2	large eggs, separated
1 teaspoon	vanilla
6 squares	(1 oz. each) semi-sweet chocolate, melted
1 cup	whipping cream

Unbaked cheesecake type desserts are quite different than baked cheesecakes, light and creamy - and really good too!

1. CRUST: Combine butter and chocolate wafer crumbs. Press into the bottom and up the sides of a 9 inch springform pan.

2. FILLING: In a large mixer bowl, beat cream cheese with sugar until smooth. Beat in egg yolks and vanilla, and then the melted chocolate.

3. Whip cream and fold into the chocolate mixture. Beat egg whites until stiff but not dry. Fold into the chocolate mixture. Pour over crust. Chill at least 4 hours before serving.

Pumpkin Cheesecake

CRUST:

⅔ cup	butter, melted
3 tablespoons	sugar
2 cups	graham wafer crumbs
¼ teaspoon	cinnamon
¼ teaspoon	nutmeg

FILLING:

2 packages	(8 oz. each) cream cheese, softened
⅔ cup	sugar
¼ cup	flour
4	large eggs
2 cups	canned pumpkin
1 teaspoon	cinnamon
¾ teaspoon	nutmeg
¼ teaspoon	allspice

A delicious fall dessert - a great choice for Thanksgiving. Top with whipped cream to complete the effect.

1. CRUST: Combine all crust ingredients. Press into the bottom and up sides of a 9 inch springform pan.

2. FILLING: In a large mixer bowl, beat cream cheese and sugar until light and fluffy. Beat in flour and add eggs one at a time while beating. Stir in pumpkin, cinnamon, nutmeg and allspice. Pour over crust. Bake at 350° F. for about 1 hour and 20 minutes, until the centre is raised and set. Let cool to room temperature. Refrigerate overnight.

Baked Desserts

Rhubarb Platz

CAKE:
1½ cups	flour
½ teaspoon	salt
1 tablespoon	baking powder
¼ cup	sugar
¼ cup	butter
1	egg
½ cup	milk

FILLING:
4 cups	chopped rhubarb
½ cup	sugar

TOPPING:
1 cup	sugar
1 cup	flour
⅓ cup	butter

This is a yummy dessert, served with scoop of vanilla ice cream. It's also nice as a brunch cake.

1. CAKE: In a medium bowl combine flour, salt, baking powder and sugar. Cut in butter until crumbly.

2. Beat egg and combine with milk. Make a well in the dry ingredients and add the egg mixture all at once. Stir to make a soft dough. Spread in a greased 9 x 13 inch baking dish.

3. FILLING: In a large bowl toss rhubarb with sugar. Spoon fruit over top of batter.

4. TOPPING: In a small bowl or food processor combine sugar and flour. Cut in butter until mixture resembles coarse crumbs. Sprinkle the topping over the rhubarb. Bake at 350° F. for 45 to 50 minutes. Serve warm.

Caramel Dumplings

SAUCE:
1 cup	brown sugar
2 tablespoons	butter
1½ cups	water

BATTER:
2 tablespoons	butter
½ cup	white sugar
½ cup	milk
1 cup	flour
1 teaspoon	baking powder
Pinch	salt

My Mom made this for us all the time when I was a kid, and we were always glad she did. We liked it even better with cream poured over top.

1. SAUCE: Combine brown sugar and butter in a small saucepan. Cook over medium heat, stirring frequently, until sugar is carmelized. Slowly add the water, stirring constantly. Boil for a few minutes. Pour into a small casserole dish.

2. BATTER: Cream the butter and sugar together. Add the milk and then the dry ingredients. Mix to blend. Drop by spoonfuls into the caramel syrup. Bake at 350° F. for 20 to 30 minutes. Serve warm.

Lemon Pudding Cake

1 cup	sugar
¼ cup	flour
¼ teaspoon	salt
¼ cup	lemon juice
1 tablespoon	grated lemon rind
1 tablespoon	melted butter
1 cup	milk
2	eggs, separated

This is a nice light dessert. It separates during baking into a souffle like topping with the lemon sauce underneath. Very tasty!

1. In a medium mixing bowl combine sugar, flour and salt. Stir in lemon juice and rind, butter and milk.

2. Beat egg yolks until thick and pale, and add to the lemon mixture. Beat egg whites until stiff but not dry, and fold into the lemon mixture. Pour into a buttered 6 cup casserole. Place in a larger pan. Pour hot water to about 1 inch deep in the larger pan. Bake at 350° F. for about 40 minutes, until the topping is set and golden. Serve warm.

Rhubarb Upside Down Cake

¼ cup	butter
¾ cup	brown sugar
1 tablespoon	orange juice
4 cups	rhubarb, cut in 1 ½ inch pieces
2 cups	flour
1 tablespoon	baking powder
½ teaspoon	salt
2 tablespoons	white sugar
⅓ cup	butter
1	egg, beaten
¼ cup	orange juice
¾ cup	milk

My Dad's favourite rhubarb recipe - I used to make this one for him. There were no arguments - everyone liked it. Good served with whipped cream.

1. Preheat oven to 350° F. Place 1/4 cup butter in a 9 inch round or 8 inch square baking pan and put in the oven until the butter is melted. Remove from the oven and stir in the brown sugar and 1 tablespoon orange juice. Arrange rhubarb in rows in the sauce. Make 2 layers of rhubarb.

2. In a medium bowl or food processor mix the flour, baking powder, salt and white sugar. Cut in 1/3 cup butter until the size of small peas.

3. Mix egg, 1/4 cup orange juice and milk together. Add to the dry ingredients and mix or process until just combined. Spread batter over the rhubarb. Push it out to touch all sides of the pan and completely cover the rhubarb. Bake for 30 to 35 minutes. Test the centre of the cake with a cake tester or toothpick to ensure that it is cooked through. Cool on a rack for 10 minutes, then invert the pan over a serving plate and carefully turn it out. Serve warm.

Peach Raspberry Cobbler

DUMPLINGS:

1 cup	flour
½ cup	sugar
1 teaspoon	baking powder
¼ teaspoon	salt
1	beaten egg
¾ cup	sour cream
2 tablespoons	butter, melted

FRUIT:

⅓ cup	sugar
2 tablespoons	cornstarch
Few grains	salt
3 cups	sliced peaches
1 package	(10 oz.) frozen raspberries, thawed
	Additional sugar

A cobbler is a comfort dessert that goes way back. You can use any fruit or combination of fruits depending on your taste or what is in season.

1. DUMPLINGS: In a medium bowl combine the flour, sugar, baking powder and salt.

2. In a small bowl, mix the egg, sour cream and melted butter. Stir into the flour mixture and blend well. Set aside.

3. FRUIT: In a large saucepan, combine sugar, cornstarch and salt. Stir in the peaches and raspberries. Cook and stir until the mixture thickens. Pour into a 1 1/2 quart casserole.

4. Drop dumpling dough from a tablespoon into the hot fruit mixture, making 6 even mounds. Sprinkle dough with a little additional sugar. Bake at 350° F. for about 30 minutes, until dumplings are done. Serve warm.

Gingerbread With Lemon Sauce

CAKE:

1¾ cups	flour
1 teaspoon	baking powder
¾ teaspoon	baking soda
½ teaspoon	salt
1 teaspoon	ground ginger
½ teaspoon	cinnamon
¼ teaspoon	grated nutmeg
6 tablespoons	butter
⅔ cup	brown sugar
½ cup	molasses
1	egg
½ teaspoon	vanilla
⅔ cup	boiling water

LEMON SAUCE:

4 teaspoons	cornstarch
Few grains	salt
¼ cup	white sugar
1½ cups	boiling water
2 teaspoons	butter
1 teaspoon	grated lemon rind
2 tablespoons	lemon juice

This is an old favourite comfort dessert. The spicy gingerbread and tangy lemon flavours go great together.

1. PUDDING: Grease an 8 inch square pan. Mix the flour, baking powder, soda, salt, and spices together.

2. Cream the butter, gradually add the brown sugar and cream thoroughly. Stir in molasses. Beat egg until thick, and beat into the creamed mixture. Stir in the vanilla.

3. Add the dry ingredients to the creamed mixture a third at a time, mixing well after each addition.

4. Gradually add boiling water, stirring after each addition. Turn into prepared pan. Bake at 325° F. for about 50 minutes. Serve warm with lemon sauce.

5. LEMON SAUCE: Combine cornstarch, salt and sugar in a small saucepan. Slowly stir boiling water into the sugar mixture. Cook over low heat, stirring constantly, until the sauce is smooth and thickened. Cover and cook over very low heat or over boiling water in a double boiler, stirring occasionally, until no raw starch taste remains, about 5 to 7 minutes. Remove from heat and stir in butter and lemon juice and rind.

Chocolate Upside Down Cake

¼ cup	butter
¾ cup	brown sugar
1 tablespoon	lemon juice
2 cups	thick sliced peeled apples
1½ cups	flour
3 teaspoons	baking powder
½ teaspoon	salt
¼ cup	cocoa
½ cup	white sugar
⅓ cup	butter
¾ cup	milk
1	egg
1 teaspoon	vanilla

This was one of our family's all time favourite desserts when I was a kid. It is unusual to pair apples and chocolate, but this is really good - try it. We always had it with whipped topping on top.

1. Preheat oven to 350° F. Melt 1/4 cup butter in a 9 inch square pan in the oven. Remove and add the brown sugar and lemon juice. Arrange apples on top of the sugar mixture.

2. Mix flour, baking powder, salt, cocoa and sugar together in a medium bowl. Cut in butter until mixture looks like fine bread crumbs.

3. Beat milk, egg and vanilla together with a fork and add to the dry ingredients. Stir just enough to blend. Spoon over the apples and spread evenly.

4. Bake for about 40 minutes, until a toothpick inserted in the centre comes out clean. Set on a rack and allow to cool for 5 minutes, then turn upside down onto a serving plate. Let it sit for 2 or 3 minutes so that all the syrup mixture and apples drop out. Serve warm.

Upside Down Chocolate Pudding

PUDDING:

1 square	(1 oz.) **unsweetened chocolate**
2 tablespoons	**butter**
1 cup	**flour**
¾ cup	**white sugar**
2½ teaspoons	**baking powder**
¼ teaspoon	**salt**
½ cup	**milk**
1 teaspoon	**vanilla**
½ to ⅔ cup	**coarsely chopped nuts**

SAUCE:

¾ cup	**white sugar**
¼ cup	**brown sugar**
2 tablespoons	**cocoa**
1 cup	**cold water**

During baking, the rich chocolate sauce ends up on the bottom, with the pudding cake on top - we thought that was pretty magical!

1. PUDDING: Melt chocolate and butter, set aside.

2. Mix flour, sugar, baking powder and salt. Stir in milk and vanilla, and then chocolate mixture. Beat until smooth. Stir in nuts. Pour the batter into an 8 inch square baking dish.

3. SAUCE: Mix white and brown sugar and cocoa together. Sprinkle evenly over top of the pudding batter. Pour the water evenly over all. Bake at 350° F. for 40 to 50 minutes. Serve warm.

Rhubarb Strawberry Cobbler

FILLING:

1¼ cups	sugar
3 tablespoons	flour
1½ teaspoons	cinnamon
6 cups	coarsely chopped fresh rhubarb
3 cups	sliced fresh strawberries

TOPPING:

1½ cups	flour
3 tablespoons	sugar
1½ teaspoons	baking powder
½ teaspoon	baking soda
¼ teaspoon	salt
3 tablespoons	butter
1 cup	buttermilk

A classic dessert featuring the classic combination of strawberries and rhubarb.

1. FILLING: In a large bowl combine sugar, flour and cinnamon. Add rhubarb and strawberries and toss to coat. Spread in a 9 x 13 inch baking dish. Bake at 400° F. for 10 minutes.

2. TOPPING: In a medium bowl combine flour, sugar, baking powder, baking soda and salt. Cut in butter until mixture resembles small peas.

3. With a fork, stir in the buttermilk to form a soft dough. Drop dough by tablespoon over the hot filling. Make 12 mounds. Bake at 400° F. for about 25 minutes, until topping is golden brown and has risen.

Rhubarb Crunch

½ cup	melted butter
1 cup	flour
¾ cup	quick cooking rolled oats
¾ cup	brown sugar
1 teaspoon	cinnamon
½ teaspoon	salt
4 cups	chopped rhubarb
¾ cup	white sugar
2 tablespoons	cornstarch
1 cup boiling	water
1 teaspoon	vanilla

This was my favourite rhubarb dessert when I was a kid. It wasn't my Mom's though, so I would rush out to the rhubarb patch and pick a bunch of rhubarb to convince her to make it. We would have it with Carnation milk poured over top, or ice cream if we were really lucky.

1. In a medium bowl combine melted butter, flour, rolled oats, brown sugar, cinnamon and salt. Mix until crumbly. Press half of the mixture into an 8 or 9 inch baking dish. Arrange rhubarb over top of the crumb mixture.

2. In a small saucepan mix the white sugar and cornstarch. Stir in the boiling water. Cook and stir until thick. Remove from heat and stir in vanilla.

3. Pour syrup evenly over the rhubarb. Sprinkle remaining crumb mixture over top. Bake at 325° F. for 50 to 60 minutes, until topping is golden and the rhubarb is tender. Serve warm.

Apple Brown Betty

PUDDING:

11	medium sized apples, preferably Spy
2 teaspoons	cinnamon
1½ cups	flour
¾ cup	brown sugar
½ cup	butter

SYRUP:

⅔ cup	brown sugar
¼ cup	hot water
	Juice of ½ lemon

This recipe is from Toby's Goodeats restaurant in Toronto, where it was a famous menu item for many, many years. Best served with ice cream.

1. PUDDING: Core and slice apples in eighths. (Peel them too if you prefer.) Spread them over the bottom of a lightly greased 8 x 12 inch baking pan. Sprinkle cinnamon over the apples.

2. To make topping, mix the flour and brown sugar together, cut in the butter until crumbly. Set aside.

3. SYRUP: Mix brown sugar with the hot water and lemon juice. Pour half of the syrup over the apples. Sprinkle the topping mixture evenly over top. Pour the remaining syrup over the topping. Bake at 350° F. for 60 minutes. Serve warm.

Creamy Top of Stove Rice Pudding

1¼ cups	water
¾ teaspoon	salt
½ cup	raw long grain rice
½ to 1 cup	raisins
½ cup	sugar
6 tablespoons	flour
⅜ teaspoon	salt
2½ cups	milk
3	large egg yolks, slightly beaten
1½ teaspoons	vanilla
⅛ teaspoon	nutmeg
⅛ teaspoon	cinnamon

Rice pudding must be the ultimate comfort dessert, full of childhood memories. Serve sprinkled with additional cinnamon.

1. Bring water and salt to a boil in a small pot. Add rice and stir. Cover, reduce heat and simmer for 30 minutes until tender. Add raisins during the last 10 or 15 minutes to plump them.

2. Meanwhile, in top of double boiler combine sugar, flour and 3/8 teaspoon salt. Stir in milk slowly, mixing after each addition so there are no lumps. Cook, stirring constantly, until thickened.

3. Add a small amount of the cooked milk mixture to the egg yolks, stirring as you add it. Then stir the egg yolks into the milk mixture in the double boiler and cook for 10 minutes. Remove from heat and stir in rice, raisins, vanilla, nutmeg and cinnamon. Serve warm or cold.

Honey Apple Crisp

6 cups	apples (2 pounds)
1 tablespoon	lemon juice
½ cup	honey
⅓ cup	flour
⅔ cup	rolled oats
½ cup	brown sugar
¼ teaspoon	salt
⅓ cup	butter

My Dad and I found this recipe when I was a kid, in a honey publication. It was a special treat to make because it was "our recipe".

1. Peel and slice apples. Arrange in a greased baking dish. Sprinkle with lemon juice. Spread honey over top.
2. Mix flour, rolled oats, brown sugar and salt together. Cut in butter until mixture looks like coarse bread crumbs. Sprinkle evenly over top of apples. Bake at 375° F. for 45 to 50 minutes, until the apples are cooked and the crust is nice and brown. Serve warm.

Bread Pudding

3	eggs, beaten
¾ cup	sugar
1 teaspoon	vanilla
¼ teaspoon	salt
3½ cups	milk
	Enough bread cubes to thicken
1 cup	raisins
	Cinnamon

Use stale bread - homemade bread is best. If you use raisin bread you can eliminate the extra raisins. You can serve it with cream but it's really good with a vanilla or rum flavoured sauce, or a fruit sauce.

1. Mix eggs, sugar, vanilla, salt and milk together. Pour into a large buttered baking dish. A
2. dd enough bread cubes to thicken (about 4 cups). Stir in raisins. Sprinkle top with cinnamon. Bake at 325° F. for 45 to 50 minutes, until the pudding is puffed up and brown, and a knife inserted in the centre comes out clean. Serve warm.

Pineapple Upside Down Cake

⅓ cup	butter
1 cup	brown sugar
9 slices	canned pineapple
9	maraschino cherries
1¾ cups	flour
1 tablespoon	baking powder
½ teaspoon	salt
½ cup	butter
1 cup	white sugar
2	eggs
1 teaspoon	vanilla
¾ cup	milk

A classic comfort dessert. Serve with whipped cream.

1. Preheat oven to 350° F. Melt 1/3 cup of butter in a 9 inch square cake pan in the oven. Remove from oven and stir in the brown sugar.
2. Arrange pineapple slices on top of the sugar, and put a cherry inside of each pineapple ring. Set aside.
3. In a small bowl combine flour, baking powder and salt. Set aside.
4. In a medium bowl cream remaining butter and sugar. Add eggs one at a time and continue beating until light. Stir in vanilla.
5. Alternate additions of dry ingredients and milk to the creamed mixture, beginning and ending with dry ingredients. Pour over the pineapple in the cake pan. Bake for 50 to 60 minutes, until toothpick inserted in the centre comes out clean. Cool for 10 minutes, then turn upside down over a serving plate. Leave the pan on top of the cake for 2 to 3 minutes to let all the syrup and fruit drop out. Serve warm.

Carrot Pudding

PUDDING:

1 cup	beef suet, ground (or ¾ cup butter)
1 cup	brown sugar
1 cup	grated potato
1 cup	grated carrot
1 cup	peeled and grated apple
2 cups	flour
1 teaspoon	baking soda
1 teaspoon	salt
1 teaspoon	cinnamon
½ teaspoon	allspice
1 cup	raisins
1 cup	currants

BROWN SUGAR SAUCE:

1 cup	brown sugar
2 tablespoons	cornstarch
¼ teaspoon	salt
2 cups	warm water
2 tablespoons	butter
2 teaspoons	vanilla

Christmas dinner would not be complete without carrot pudding for dessert.

1. PUDDING: Mix suet, brown sugar, potato, carrot and apple together.

2. In a large bowl combine the flour, baking soda, salt and spices. Add the suet mixture and blend well. Stir in raisins and currants. Spoon into a greased 10 cup pudding mold. Cover with foil and tie with string. Or you can use coffee tins, for smaller puddings.

3. Put in steamer - boiling water should be half way up the side of the pudding tin. Steam for 3 to 4 hours, adding more water as required. Remove from heat, cool, wrap and refrigerate for a few weeks to let the flavour blend. Before serving, heat by re-steaming until heated through, or heat in the microwave.

4. BROWN SUGAR SAUCE: Combine brown sugar, cornstarch and salt in a saucepan. Add warm water gradually, stirring constantly. Cook and stir over low heat, until thick and smooth (about 3 to 5 minutes). Remove from heat, add butter and vanilla. Serve hot.

Chilled Desserts

Khalua Mousse Torte

1 cup	milk
2 tablespoons	Khalua (coffee) liqueur
1 package	Chips Ahoy chocolate chip cookies
2 packages	Dream Whip topping, prepared as directed

No one will believe that such a fancy cake was whipped up in minutes from a package of cookies (so don't tell them!)

1. Combine milk and Khalua in a small bowl. Dip cookies in the milk mixture and then arrange them on the bottom of a 9 inch springform pan in a single layer.

2. When you have covered the bottom of the pan with cookies, top with a layer of Dream Whip. Continue with layers of dipped cookies and Dream Whip. End with Dream Whip layer. Decorate the top with chocolate shavings or curls. Refrigerate several hours or overnight. Remove from the springform to a fancy cake plate to serve.

Oreo Ice Cream Pie

1 cup	finely crushed Oreo cookies (about 12 cookies)
3 tablespoons	melted butter
3	egg yolks
1 can	sweetened condensed milk
4 teaspoons	vanilla
1 cup	coarsely crushed Oreo cookies (about 12 cookies)
2 cups	whipping cream, whipped

This is so good, better than a restaurant dessert! You can make the ice cream alone too. Omit the crumb crust, freeze in a 2 quart container and spoon into bowls to serve.

1. Mix 1 cup crushed Oreo crumbs with melted butter. Spread in the bottom of a 9 inch springform pan.

2. In a large bowl, beat egg yolks until light. Stir in sweetened condensed milk and vanilla. Fold in Oreo crumbs and whipped cream. Pour over the crust. Freeze for 6 hours or overnight. Garnish with more Oreo cookies if desired, or serve with chocolate sauce.

Cherry Cha-Cha Pudding

1½ cups	graham wafer crumbs
⅓ cup	melted butter
1 cup	whipping cream
4 cups	miniature marshmallows
1 can	cherry pie filling

This was a huge favourite at my house when I was a kid.

1. Combine graham wafer crumbs and melted butter. Reserve about 1/3 of a cup of the mixture, and spread the rest in the bottom of a 9 inch square pan.

2. Whip the cream and mix with the marshmallows. Spread half of this mixture over the crumb crust. Top with the cherry pie filling, then the rest of the cream mixture. Sprinkle the reserved crumb mixture over the top. Chill overnight. Cut into squares to serve.

Crispy Crunch Torte

1	angel food cake
2 cups	whipping cream
8	Crispy Crunch chocolate bars

A decadent special occasion dessert that kids will love (adults too!)

1. Cut the angel food cake into 3 layers. Whip cream until stiff.

2. Coarsely chop the Crispy Crunch bars in the food processor. Reserve about 1/2 cup of the crumbs to sprinkle on top. Fold the rest into the whipped cream.

3. Place the bottom cake layer on a serving plate. Top with some of the whipped cream mixture. Top with the next layer, more whipped cream mixture, then the top layer. Ice the top and sides with the remaining whipped cream mixture. Refrigerate for at least 3 hours. Top with reserved Crispy Crunch crumbs before serving.

Lemon Dessert Cake

1	angel food cake
1 cup	whipping cream, whipped
1	lemon pie filling mix, cooked and cooled

Buy an angel food cake from the bakery and turn it into a fancy homemade dessert! You can also make the cake from a mix or even from scratch.

1. Slice angel food cake horizontally into 3 layers. Fold whipped cream into the lemon pie filling mix until smooth.

2. Place bottom cake layer on a cake plate. Spread some of the lemon mixture over. Top with the next cake layer. Spread some lemon mixture over. Top with the top cake layer. Ice the top and sides of the cake with the remaining lemon mixture. Refrigerate several hours or overnight.

Aloha Pineapple Squares

2½ cups	graham wafer crumbs
½ cup	melted butter
¼ cup	sugar
1 teaspoon	cinnamon
½ cup	butter
1½ cups	icing (confectioners') sugar
2	egg yolks
1 cup	whipping cream
1 can	(19 oz.) crushed pineapple, drained

This is one of my favourite summertime desserts from when I was a kid. A great "make and take" dessert for a barbecue.

1. Mix graham wafer crumbs, melted butter, sugar and cinnamon. Reserve 3/4 cup of this mixture for topping. Press the rest into an 8 x 12 inch pan. Bake at 350° F. for 12 minutes. Cool.

2. With mixer cream butter and icing sugar. Add egg yolks and beat until light. Spread over the cooled crust.

3. Beat whipping cream until stiff. Fold in pineapple. Spread over the second layer in the pan. Sprinkle the reserved crumb mixture over top. Chill for several hours or overnight. Cut into squares to serve.

Strawberry Dessert

1½ cups	graham wafer crumbs
¼ cup	sugar
¼ cup	melted butter
1	strawberry jelly powder
1 cup	boiling water
1 package	(10 oz.) frozen strawberries, partially thawed
20	large marshmallows
½ cup	milk
1 cup	whipping cream, whipped

This is a pretty dessert. We used to make it back home with raspberries (frozen from the summer's crop from the garden) and raspberry jelly powder - which made it Raspberry Dessert. It was a picnic favourite.

1. Mix graham wafer crumbs, sugar and melted butter together. Reserve about 1/4 cup of the crumbs and spread the rest in the bottom of a 9 x 13 inch pan.

2. Mix jelly powder and boiling water. Chill until slightly set, then stir in the strawberries. Pour over the crumb crust.

3. Melt the marshmallows and milk together. Let cool. Fold in the whipped cream. Spread over the strawberry layer. Top with the reserved crumb mixture. Refrigerate several hours or overnight. Cut into squares to serve.

Extra Recipes

Cookies, Squares & Candy

Cookies

Oatmeal Raisin Cookies

2¼ cups	flour
½ teaspoon	baking soda
¼ teaspoon	salt
1 cup	oatmeal
1 cup	butter, softened
1 cup	dark brown sugar
½ cup	white sugar
2	eggs
2 tablespoons	liquid honey
2 teaspoons	vanilla
1½ cups	raisins
½ cup	chopped walnuts

These are really delicious. Don't overcook them and they will be nice and chewy. If you prefer you can omit the nuts and increase the raisins to 2 cups.

1. Mix flour, baking soda, salt and oatmeal together.
2. Cream butter and sugars. Add eggs and beat well. Stir in honey and vanilla. Add flour mixture and mix. Stir in raisins and nuts. Drop by tablespoonfuls 2 inches apart on ungreased cookie sheets. Bake at 300° F. for 18 to 22 minutes. Remove from cookie sheet to cool.

Quick Coconut Oatmeal Cookies

1¼ cups	flour
1 teaspoon	baking powder
1 teaspoon	baking soda
½ teaspoon	salt
½ cup	white sugar
½ cup	brown sugar
½ cup	butter, softened
1	egg
1 teaspoon	vanilla
1 cup	oatmeal
1 cup	coconut

You mix all the batter ingredients up in one bowl - hence they are "quick". And they are also very good - a nice crisp oatmeal cookie with the tasty addition of coconut.

1. Mix flour, baking powder, baking soda and salt in a large mixing bowl. Add sugars, butter and egg. Mix until smooth. Stir in vanilla. Fold in oatmeal and coconut. Shape into balls and place 2 inches apart on ungreased cookie sheet. Bake at 350° F. for 12 to 15 minutes.

Chocolate Chip Cookies

1 cup	butter, softened
½ cup	white sugar
1 cup	dark brown sugar
2	eggs
2 teaspoons	vanilla
2½ cups	flour
½ teaspoon	baking soda
½ teaspoon	salt
2 cups	chocolate chips

Is there anything better than a homemade chocolate chip cookie, fresh out of the oven?

1. Cream butter and sugars. Add eggs, and continue to beat until light and fluffy. Add vanilla.
2. Mix flour, baking soda and salt together. Gradually add to creamed mixture and stir until combined. Stir in chocolate chips. Drop by spoonfuls onto ungreased cookie sheet. Bake at 300° F. for 18 to 24 minutes.

Peanut Butter Cookies

1 cup	butter, softened
1¼ cups	dark brown sugar
1¼ cups	white sugar
3	eggs
1 cup	smooth peanut butter
2 teaspoons	vanilla
2 cups	flour
½ teaspoon	baking soda
¼ teaspoon	salt

Peanut butter cookies are certainly a classic comfort food.

1. Cream butter and sugars. Add eggs, and beat in. Add peanut butter and continue to beat until light and fluffy. Add vanilla.
2. Mix flour, baking soda and salt together. Gradually add to creamed mixture and stir until combined. Shape dough into balls and place on ungreased cookie sheet, about 2 inches apart. Flatten cookies with a fork, making a criss cross pattern on the tops. Bake at 300° F. for 18 to 22 minutes.

Boston Cookies

1 cup butter, softened
1 cup sugar
2 eggs
1 teaspoon vanilla
2 cups flour
½ teaspoon baking powder
½ teaspoon baking soda
2 cups dates, cut up
½ cup chopped walnuts

My Grandma's recipe for soft, chewy and delicious cookies.

1. Cream butter and sugar. Add eggs, and continue to beat until light and fluffy. Add vanilla.
2. Mix flour, baking powder and baking soda together. Gradually add to creamed mixture and stir until combined. Stir in dates and walnuts. Drop by spoonfuls onto ungreased cookie sheet. Bake at 350° F. for about 15 minutes.

Molasses Cookies

½ cup	molasses
5 teaspoons	baking soda
2½ cups	flour
2½ cups	sugar
1 teaspoon	salt
1 teaspoon	cinnamon
½ teaspoon	nutmeg
2½ cups	oatmeal
¾ cup	butter
¾ cup	shortening
2	eggs

This is my Auntie Bess's recipe, and one of my favourite comfort foods.

1. Heat molasses in microwave or on the stove. Stir in baking soda. Set aside. Note: the baking soda makes it puff up, so heat in a larger bowl.
2. Mix flour, sugar, salt, cinnamon, nutmeg and oatmeal in a large bowl. Cut in butter and shortening until crumbly. Stir in molasses. Add unbeaten eggs. Mix well. Roll in balls. Arrange on ungreased cookie sheet 2 inches apart. Bake at 350° F. for 10 to 15 minutes.

Grandma's Shortbread Cookies

2 cups	**butter**
1 cup	**brown sugar**
¼ teaspoon	**salt**
4 cups	**flour**

For our family, the sure sign that Christmas was coming was when the very first batch of shortbread cookies appeared at Grandma's! Her Cornish shortbread recipe uses brown sugar, which adds a nice flavour.

1. Bring butter to room temperature. Cream the butter until it is the consistency of whipped cream. Beat in the sugar. Add salt. Add flour in 4 portions (one cup at a time) mixing well after each addition. Turn out onto a floured board and pat or roll to 1/4 to 1/2 inch thick. Cut into shape desired with a cookie cutter. Place on an ungreased cookie sheet and bake at 300° F. for about 20 minutes, or until lightly browned.

Chocolate Shortbread

1 cup	**butter**
¾ cup	**icing (confectioners') sugar**
1½ cups	**flour**
	Few grains salt
⅓ cup	**cocoa**

This recipe, from a Fry's Cocoa booklet I sent away for when I was a kid, quickly became a family Christmas favourite.

1. Soften butter to room temperature. Cream butter until soft and fluffy. Beat in icing sugar. Stir in flour, salt, and cocoa, and mix well. If very soft, chill in refrigerator for 1/2 hour. Shape dough into 1 inch balls and place on an ungreased cookie sheet about 2 inches apart. Flatten balls with a fork. (Or if desired, you can roll out the dough to 1/4 to 1/2 inch thick and cut with a cookie cutter.) Bake at 300° F. for 20 to 25 minutes. Remove from oven, cool slightly and remove from pan.

Thimble Cookies

½ cup	butter
¼ cup	brown sugar
1	egg yolk
1 teaspoon	vanilla
1 cup	flour
1	egg white
¾ cup	chopped walnuts
½ cup	jam or jelly

Another one of Grandma's Christmas cookie recipes. They're called thimble cookies because a thimble is perfect for making the indent in the centre.

1. Cream butter, add sugar and beat until fluffy. Add egg yolk, and beat well. Stir in vanilla. Add flour and stir until combined. Roll mixture into balls the size of a walnut. Roll balls in unbeaten egg white, then in chopped walnuts.

2. Make an indent in the top of each cookie and place on a greased cookie sheet, and bake at 350° F. for 5 minutes. Remove from the oven and redent the tops of the cookies, then continue baking until done - another 5 to 10 minutes. They should be slightly brown. Fill the indents with a teaspoon of jam or jelly while they are hot, and remove to a rack or plate to cool.

Mocha Disks

½ cup	butter
1 cup	brown sugar
1	egg
1 square	(1 oz.) unsweetened chocolate, melted
1 teaspoon	vanilla
1¼ cups	flour
1 teaspoon	baking powder
¼ teaspoon	salt
2 teaspoons	instant coffee granules
¾ cup	finely chopped walnuts

From my Mom's recipe archive - a great addition to the Christmas cookie lineup, with a tasty combination of chocolate and coffee, rolled in nuts.

1. Cream butter, add sugar and cream together until light and fluffy. Add egg and beat well. Stir in chocolate and vanilla.

2. Mix together remaining ingredients, except walnuts. Stir in to the creamed mixture. Chill dough several hours or overnight. Take a teaspoon of dough and form a ball. Roll in walnuts. Place 2 inches apart on a greased cookie sheet. Bake at 375° F. for 15 minutes.

Pecan Puffs

1 cup	butter
2 tablespoons	brown sugar
2 tablespoons	white sugar
1 teaspoon	vanilla
2 cups	flour
1 cup	chopped pecans
	Additional white sugar

This is Auntie Bess's recipe for my favourite Christmas cookies.

1. Soften butter to room temperature. Cream butter, add sugar and beat until fluffy. Stir in vanilla. Add flour and stir until combined. Mix in the chopped pecans. Roll into small balls and place on an ungreased cookie sheet. Bake at 300° F. for 15 to 20 minutes, until the bottoms are golden brown.

2. Put some white sugar in a small bowl. While hot, roll each cookie in the sugar to coat, and set on a rack or plate to cool.

Chocolate Chunk Shortbread

2 cups	butter
6 oz.	bittersweet chocolate
1 cup	icing (confectioners') sugar
3½ cups	flour
½ cup	cornstarch
1 cup	coarsely chopped pecans

A very tasty Christmas cookie for the chocolate chip cookie lover.

1. Soften butter to room temperature. Coarsely chop chocolate into chunks and set aside. Cream butter and sugar until light and fluffy. Stir in flour and cornstarch and mix well. Stir in chocolate and pecan chunks. Drop dough in heaping tablespoons onto a greased cookie sheet, about an inch apart. Bake at 350° F. for 20 to 25 minutes. Remove from oven, cool slightly and remove from pan.

Cherry Flips

1 cup	butter
About 30	Marachino cherries plus juice
½ cup	icing (confectioners') sugar
2 egg	yolks
1 teaspoon	almond extract
2 cups	flour
¼ teaspoon	salt
	Additional icing sugar
	Coconut (optional)

Mom used to make these at Christmas time. They're good, with a surprise cherry inside!

1. Soften butter to room temperature. Drain cherries well (reserving juice) and dry with paper towel.
2. Cream butter and sugar. Add egg yolks and beat well. Stir in almond extract. Blend in flour and salt.
3. Pinch off a piece of dough. Press the dough in the palm of your hand and place a cherry on top. Mould the dough around the cherry to form a ball. Place balls on a greased cookie sheet and bake at 325° F. for about 25 minutes.
4. Make a thin icing with icing sugar and some of the reserved cherry juice. When cool, dip the cookie tops in icing, and dip into coconut if desired.

Irish Cream Balls

1 package	vanilla wafer cookies
¼ cup	milk chocolate
½ cup	Irish Cream liqueur
1 cup	coconut

A great treat for the holiday season. Try to hide them and forget about them for about a week to let the flavours develop. You could also coat them in cocoa, icing sugar, or more vanilla wafer crumbs instead of coconut.

1. Crush the vanilla wafers - a food processor is the fastest for this. Melt the chocolate and add to the crushed wafers, along with the liqueur. Roll into small balls and roll in coconut to coat. Refrigerate to set, then pack in containers and keep refrigerated.

Butter Balls

⅔ cup	butter
¾ cup	white sugar
3 tablespoons	cocoa
½ teaspoon	vanilla
1 tablespoon	water
2 cups	oatmeal
½ cup	icing (confectioners') sugar

Grandma made these treats for us all the time. There are claims that we kids would head straight for the fridge to find the Butter Balls without even saying hello to Grandma first.

1. Soften butter to room temperature. Cream butter and sugar. Add cocoa, vanilla, water and oatmeal, and blend well. Chill for about an hour until firm enough to handle.

2. Put icing sugar in a small bowl. Shape dough into small balls, and roll in icing sugar. Store in the fridge.

Unbaked Chocolate Cookies

3 cups	rolled oats
1 cup	coconut
½ cup	cocoa
½ teaspoon	salt
2 cups	sugar
½ cup	milk
½ cup	butter
1 teaspoon	vanilla

I used to make these a lot when I was a kid. They are almost like a candy, popular on cookie trays. A good summer cookie too when you don't feel like heating up the house by using the oven.

1. Mix rolled oats, coconut, cocoa and salt together in a large bowl. Set aside.

2. Mix sugar, milk and butter together in a saucepan and bring to a boil. Boil for 2 minutes. Remove from heat and stir in vanilla. Add dry ingredients and mix. Drop by teaspoons onto wax paper and let cool.

Java Jems

2½ cups	rolled oats
1 cup	coconut
½ teaspoon	salt
2 cups	sugar
½ cup	milk
½ cup	butter
2 teaspoons	instant coffee granules
1 teaspoon	vanilla

These are very tasty, and easy too - no baking required, so no watching the oven to see if they are done. Just cool and enjoy!

1. Mix rolled oats, coconut, and salt together in a large bowl. Set aside.
2. Mix sugar, milk, butter and instant coffee together in a saucepan and bring to a boil. Boil for 2 minutes. Remove from heat and stir in vanilla. Add dry ingredients and mix. Drop by teaspoons onto wax paper and let cool.

Date Balls

1	egg
1½ tbsp.	butter
1 cup brown	sugar
1 cup	chopped dates
1 teaspoon	vanilla
2 cups	Rice Krispies cereal
1 cup	coconut

I always made these at home for the "Christmas dainty tray". They're attractive and they're yummy too!

1. Mix together in a heavy pot the egg, butter, brown sugar and dates. Cook and stir over medium heat until thick and smooth. Remove from heat and stir in vanilla. Allow to cool slightly. Stir in Rice Krispies. Roll mixture into small balls and roll in coconut.

Baked Squares

Dream Bars

BASE:

2 tablespoons	icing (confectioners') sugar
1 cup	flour
½ cup	butter

TOPPING:

2	eggs
1 cup	brown sugar
¼ cup	flour
1 teaspoon	baking powder
⅛ teaspoon	salt
1 teaspoon	vanilla
1 cup	chopped walnuts
1 cup	coconut

Rich and delicious - they aren't called dream bars for nothing.

1. BASE: Combine icing sugar and flour. Cut in butter until fine and mealy - use food processor or blend with a pastry blender. Pat into a greased 8 inch square pan. Bake for 20 minutes at 300° F.

2. TOPPING: Beat eggs well, and add sugar.

3. Mix flour, baking powder and salt together. Add to the egg mixture and stir. Add vanilla, walnuts, and coconut. Spread over the base. Bake at 300° F. for 30 to 35 minutes. The topping will be very soft when removed from the oven, but it becomes firm as it cools. Do not try to cut or remove from the pan until cold.

Matrimonial Cake

BASE:
2 cups	oatmeal
2 cups	flour
1 cup	brown sugar
1 teaspoon	baking powder
½ teaspoon	baking soda
½ teaspoon	salt
1 cup	butter

DATE FILLING:
½ pound	dates, pitted
⅔ cup	water
¼ cup	white sugar
1 teaspoon	lemon juice

This is an old time favourite recipe that my Mom and my Grandma used to make all the time.

1. BASE: In a large bowl, combine oatmeal, flour, brown sugar, baking powder, baking soda and salt. Cut in butter until crumbly. Spread 3/4 of the crumbs in a 9 x 13 inch cake pan.

2. DATE FILLING: Mix dates, water and sugar together in a saucepan. Cook until thick, stirring frequently. Remove from heat and add lemon juice. Allow to cool before using.

3. Spread filling over the crumbs in the pan. Sprinkle the remaining crumbs over top of the filling. Bake at 350° F. for 20 minutes. Cool and cut in squares.

Pumpkin Squares

CAKE:

½ cup	butter
½ cup	white sugar
½ cup	brown sugar
2	eggs
1 can	(14 oz.) pumpkin
1 cup	flour
1 teaspoon	cinnamon
¼ teaspoon	nutmeg
¼ teaspoon	ginger
1 teaspoon	baking powder
½ teaspoon	baking soda
¼ teaspoon	salt

ICING:

1 package	(4 oz.) cream cheese, softened
¼ cup	butter
1 teaspoon	vanilla
2 cups	icing (confectioners') sugar

Moist delicious squares that taste like pumpkin pie! Nice for a Thanksgiving or fall treat.

1. CAKE: In a large mixer bowl, cream butter and sugars together. Beat in eggs. Add pumpkin and stir to blend.

2. In a small bowl, combine flour with the remaining dry ingredients. Stir together, then add to the creamed mixture. Stir to blend. Spread in a greased 9 x 13 inch pan. Bake for 25 minutes at 350° F. Remove from oven, and allow to cool.

3. ICING: Beat cream cheese and butter together, until smooth. Stir in vanilla. Gradually add icing sugar and beat until smooth. Spread over the cooled cake, chill and cut into squares.

Honey Date Bars

1 cup	liquid honey
3	eggs, beaten
1 teaspoon	vanilla
1⅓ cups	flour
1 teaspoon	baking powder
½ teaspoon	salt
3 cups	chopped dates
½ cup	chopped walnuts

A tasty chewy bar - very simple to prepare.

1. Combine honey, eggs and vanilla and beat well to blend.
2. Combine flour, baking powder and salt. Add to honey mixture and stir to combine. Stir in dates and nuts. Spread in a greased 9 x 13 inch baking pan. Bake for 45 minutes at 350° F. until nicely browned and top springs back when touched lightly.

Peanut Butter Bars

BASE:
¾ cup butter
⅓ cup peanut butter
1 cup brown sugar
1 egg, beaten
1 teaspoon vanilla
2 cups flour

ICING:
1 cup chocolate chips
½ cup peanut butter

Chocolate and peanut butter - a great combination!

1. BASE: Cream butter, peanut butter and brown sugar together. Blend in egg and vanilla. Add flour and mix well. Spread in a 10 x 15 inch jelly roll pan. Bake for 15 to 20 minutes at 350° F. Remove from oven.
2. ICING: Melt chocolate chips and peanut butter together. Spread over base. Cool and cut into squares.

Jam Squares

1 cup plus 2 tablespoons	flour
½ cup	sugar
1 teaspoon	baking powder
⅛ teaspoon	salt
	Grated rind of 1 lemon
⅓ cup	butter
1	egg, beaten
½ cup	raspberry jam

Jam is a classic ingredient in squares - this is a simple jam square. For variety, you can use different jams for the filling.

1. Combine flour, sugar, baking powder, salt and lemon rind in food processor bowl. Add butter and process until mixture resembles coarse meal. Add egg and process briefly to combine.

2. Spread 2/3 of the mixture in a greased 8 inch square baking pan. Pat down firmly. Spread jam over top, and sprinkle remaining batter over jam. Bake for 25 minutes at 350° F. until well browned. Cool and cut into squares.

Chocolate Chews

¾ cup plus 2 tablespoons	flour
1 teaspoon	baking powder
¼ teaspoon	salt
¾ cup	sugar
1	egg
½ cup	butter, softened
2 squares	(1 oz. each) unsweetened chocolate, melted
½ teaspoon	vanilla
¾ cups	quick cooking rolled oats
¼ cup	chopped walnuts

This is a simple and quick recipe - perfect when you need to whip up a treat in a hurry.

1. In a medium mixing bowl, combine flour, baking powder, salt and sugar. Stir in egg, butter, chocolate and vanilla. Beat until smooth. Stir in rolled oats and walnuts. Spread in a greased 8 inch square baking pan. Bake for 30 minutes at 325° F. until top springs back when touched. Cool and cut into squares.

Raspberry Dream Bars

BASE:
1½ cups	flour
1 teaspoon	baking soda
¼ cup	brown sugar
¼ cup	white sugar
½ cup	butter
1	egg
1 tablespoon	milk
½ cup	raspberry jam

TOPPING:
2 tablespoons	butter
1 cup	white sugar
2	eggs, separated
¼ teaspoon	salt
1 teaspoon	vanilla
1 cup	chopped walnuts

Mmmmm, dreamy, with raspberry jam.

1. BASE: Combine flour, baking soda, and sugars. Cut in butter - use food processor or blend with a pastry blender.

2. Beat egg and milk together. Make a well in the dry ingredients and pour in the milk mixture. Mix to combine.

3. Pat into a greased 9 inch square pan. Bake for 12 to 15 minutes at 375° F. Remove from oven and spread jam over top. Reduce oven temperature to 350° F.

4. TOPPING: Cream butter and sugar together. Beat in egg yolks. Add salt, vanilla and chopped walnuts.

5. Beat egg whites until stiff. Fold into the creamed mixture. Spread evenly over the jam. Bake at 350° F. for 25 to 30 minutes. Cool and cut into squares.

Maple Walnut Squares

BASE:
1 cup	flour
¼ cup	brown sugar
½ cup	butter, softened

TOPPING:
⅔ cup	brown sugar
1 cup	maple syrup
2	eggs, beaten
¼ cup	butter, softened
¼ teaspoon	salt
½ teaspoon	vanilla
2 tablespoons	flour
⅔ cup	walnut halves

Maple syrup and walnuts go so well together in these rich tasty squares. They are great on their own, or try them with a scoop of ice cream for dessert.

1. BASE: Rub flour, brown sugar and butter together. Press into a 9 inch square pan. Bake at 350° F. for 5 minutes.

2. TOPPING: Combine sugar and maple syrup in a saucepan, simmer 5 minutes. Remove from heat and cool slightly. Pour over beaten eggs, stirring well. Stir in butter, salt, vanilla and flour.

3. Spread walnut halves evenly over base. Pour maple syrup mixture over walnuts. Bake at 450° F. for 10 minutes. Reduce heat to 350° F. and bake for 20 minutes. Cool and cut into squares.

Granola Bars

3 cups	rolled oats
1 cup	nuts, coarsely chopped
1 cup	dried fruit
1 cup	raw unsalted sunflower seeds
1 can	sweetened condensed milk
½ cup	butter, melted

These homemade granola bars are so easy to make, and so tasty too. You can make different varieties by using different fruits (e.g. raisins, chopped dates, dried apple, dried cherries, dried cranberries, chopped dried apricots) and nuts (e.g. almonds, pecans, walnuts). They are great for snacks and to pack in lunches.

1. Combine all ingredients in a large bowl and mix well. Line a 10 x 15 inch baking pan with foil and grease the foil. Spoon batter into the pan. Bake at 325° F. for 25 to 30 minutes, until golden brown. Cool slightly, remove from pan, peel off foil and cut into bars.

Almond Roca Squares

BASE:

½ cup	butter, softened
¼ cup	white sugar
¼ cup	brown sugar
½ teaspoon	vanilla
1	egg yolk
½ cup	flour
½ cup	rolled oats

ICING:

8 oz.	milk chocolate bar
1 teaspoon	butter
½ cup	ground almonds

This recipe is from my Auntie Bess. With a chocolate bar icing, these are so good!

1. BASE: Combine all ingredients. Pat into a greased 8 inch square pan. Bake for 20 minutes at 350° F. Remove from oven and let cool.
2. ICING: Coarsely chop chocolate. Melt chocolate and butter together. Spread over cooled base. Sprinkle ground almonds over top. Cut into squares. Keep in the fridge.

Rocky Road Bars

BASE:

3 squares	(1 oz. each) semi-sweet chocolate
½ cup	butter
1½ cups	graham wafer crumbs
½ cup	finely chopped pecans
½ cup	flaked coconut

TOPPING:

1½ cups	miniature marshmallows
1 cup	flaked coconut
1 cup	pecans
1 can	sweetened condensed milk
3 squares	(1 oz. each) semi-sweet chocolate

A yummy square recipe with the classic "rocky road" combination of chocolate, marshmallows and nuts. Quick and easy to make.

1. BASE: Preheat oven to 350° F. Put chocolate and butter in a 9 x 13 inch cake pan. Put in the oven to melt. Remove from the oven and add the graham wafer crumbs, pecans and coconut. Mix well and then press into the bottom of the pan.

2. TOPPING: Sprinkle marshmallows over base. Sprinkle coconut over marshmallows, and then pecans. Pour the sweetened condensed milk evenly over all. Bake for 25 to 30 minutes until golden brown. Remove from oven and cool. Melt chocolate squares. Drizzle over the cooled bars. Chill and cut into squares.

Oh Henry Bars

BASE:
⅔ cup	butter
1 cup	brown sugar
4 cups	rolled oats
½ cup	corn syrup
3 teaspoons	vanilla
Pinch	salt

ICING:
1 cup	chocolate chips
⅔ cup	peanut butter

I started making these when I was a kid - they are yummy.

1. BASE: Cream butter and sugar. Add rolled oats, syrup, vanilla and salt. Blend well. Press into a 9 x 13 inch pan. Bake for 10 to 12 minutes at 375° F. Do not overbake or it will turn rock hard. Remove from oven and let cool.

2. ICING: Melt chocolate chips and peanut butter together. Spread over cooled base. Cut into squares. Keep in the fridge.

Hello Dollies

½ cup	butter
1½ cups	graham wafer crumbs
1 cup	chopped walnuts
1 cup	chocolate chips
1½ cups	flaked coconut
1 can	sweetened condensed milk

These are also known as 6 Layer Bars - because the 6 ingredients in the recipe are layered one by one in the pan. You can't get much easier than that, and they are so good, too.

1. Preheat oven to 350° F. Put butter in a 9 x 13 inch cake pan and place in the oven until the butter is melted. Remove from oven, and spread the melted butter evenly over the bottom of the pan.

2. Sprinkle the graham wafer crumbs evenly over the melted butter. Sprinkle walnuts over the graham wafer crumbs, then chocolate chips, then coconut. Pour sweetened condensed milk evenly over top of the coconut. Return to oven and bake for about 25 minutes, until lightly browned on top. Cut into small squares when cooled.

Chocolate Pecan Squares

BASE:

½ cup	butter, softened
1	egg yolk
1	cup flour
2 tablespoons	icing (confectioners') sugar

TOPPING:

3	eggs
½ cup	brown sugar
2 tablespoons	flour
¼ teaspoon	salt
⅔ cup	corn syrup
1 tablespoon	lemon juice
1 cup	pecans
1 cup	chocolate chips

If you like pecan pie, you will love these squares.

1. BASE: Combine butter and egg yolk in a mixing bowl. Add flour and icing sugar. Press into a greased 8 inch square pan. Bake at 350° F. for 15 minutes.

2. TOPPING: In a large bowl, beat eggs until slightly foamy.

3. Combine brown sugar, flour, and salt. Stir into the eggs until blended. Beat in the corn syrup and lemon juice. Stir in the pecans and chocolate chips. Spread over the base. Bake. for 35 to 40 minutes, until the top is set and the edges are browned. Cut into squares when cold.

Cherry Slice

BASE:
¾ cup	butter, softened
2 tablespoons	white sugar
1½ cups	flour

TOPPING:
2	eggs
1½ cups	brown sugar
2 tablespoons	flour
1 teaspoon	baking powder
½ cup	coconut
½ cup	chopped walnuts
1 cup	candied cherries

Use a combination of red and green cherries to make these extra festive for Christmas.

1. BASE: Combine butter, sugar and flour. Pat into a 9 inch square cake pan. Bake at 300° F. for 10 minutes.

2. TOPPING: Beat eggs. Add brown sugar and beat together. Stir in flour and baking powder. Add coconut, walnuts and cherries. Pour over the base. Bake for 30 minutes. Cool and cut into squares.

Brownies

Chocolate Cheesecake Brownies

BROWNIES:

½ cup	butter
4 squares	(1 oz. each) semi-sweet chocolate
2	eggs
1 cup	brown sugar
¾ cup	flour
¼ teaspoon	baking powder
⅓ cup	coarsely chopped pecans

CHEESECAKE TOPPING:

1 package	(8 oz.) cream cheese, softened
½ cup	white sugar
2 tablespoons	butter, softened
2	eggs
2 tablespoons	milk
1 tablespoon	flour
3 squares	(1 oz. each) semi-sweet chocolate, finely chopped

ICING:

¼ cup	sugar
¼ cup	whipping cream
½ teaspoon	vanilla
2 squares	(1 oz. each) semi-sweet chocolate
2 tablespoons	butter

These are very good, more like a dessert than a square.

1. BROWNIES: Melt butter and chocolate together. Set aside to cool. In a large mixing bowl, beat the eggs and sugar together until light. Stir in the flour and baking powder, and the cooled chocolate mixture. Fold in pecans. Pour into a greased 9 inch square pan.

2. CHEESECAKE TOPPING: In a large bowl, beat together cream cheese, sugar and butter until creamy. Beat in eggs, milk and flour. Stir in chopped chocolate. Spread over brownie layer in pan. Bake at 350° F. for 40 to 45 minutes. Cool.

3. ICING: Combine sugar, cream and vanilla in a small saucepan. Stir to blend. Place over medium high heat and bring to a boil. Reduce heat and simmer for 5 minutes without stirring. Remove from heat and add chocolate and butter. Stir until chocolate has melted and mixture is slightly cooled and thick enough to spread. Pour over cooled cake. Chill and cut into squares. Store in refrigerator.

Basic Brownies

½ cup	butter
2 squares	(1 oz. each) unsweetened chocolate
1 cup	sugar
2	eggs, well beaten
½ teaspoon	vanilla
¾ cup	flour
¼ teaspoon	salt
½ cup	chopped walnuts

Sometimes you just want a basic brownie - these are very quick, easy and yummy.

1. Melt butter and chocolate together in a large saucepan. Remove from heat and stir in remaining ingredients. Pour into a greased 8 inch square pan. Bake at 350° F. for 25 to 30 minutes. Cool and cut into squares.

Triple Chocolate Brownies

BROWNIES:

⅓ cup	butter
3 squares	(1 oz. each) unsweetened chocolate
⅔ cup	flour
½ teaspoon	baking powder
¼ teaspoon	salt
2	eggs
¾ cup	sugar
1 teaspoon	vanilla
1 cup	white chocolate chips

ICING:

4 oz.	milk chocolate
3 tablespoons	butter

All the chocolate bases are covered with this attractive and tasty brownie treat.

1. BROWNIES: Melt butter and chocolate together. Set aside to cool. In a small bowl, combine flour, baking powder and salt. In a large bowl beat eggs. Blend in sugar. Add chocolate mixture and vanilla. Stir in flour mixture, and white chocolate chips. Pour into a greased 8 inch square pan. Bake at 325° F. for 18 to 20 minutes. Cool.

2. ICING: Melt milk chocolate and butter together. Spread over the cooled cake. Cool and cut into squares. Store in refrigerator.

Blonde Brownies

BROWNIES:

⅓ cup	butter
1½ cups	brown sugar
2	eggs, beaten
1 teaspoon	vanilla
1 cup	flour
1 teaspoon	baking powder
½ teaspoon	salt
1 cup	chopped walnuts
½ cup	chocolate chips

BROWNED BUTTER ICING:

1½ tbsp.	butter
1½ cups	icing (confectioners') sugar
¾ teaspoon	vanilla
	Light cream

A different kind of brownie - kind of like a nice soft chocolate chip cookie in a bar. Yummy!

1. BROWNIES: Melt butter, stir in sugar, eggs and vanilla.

2. In a small bowl mix flour, baking powder and salt. Add to the butter mixture and blend well. Stir in nuts and chocolate chips. Pour into a greased 9 inch square pan. Bake at 350° F. for about 30 minutes, until the top springs back when touched lightly.

3. BROWNED BUTTER ICING: Put butter in a small saucepan and heat until golden brown. Remove from heat and add icing sugar, vanilla, and enough cream to make a mixture that is easy to spread. Spread on cooled cake. Cut into squares.

Mochachino Brownies

BROWNIES:

½ cup	butter
4 squares	(1 oz. each) **unsweetened chocolate**
1 tablespoon	instant coffee powder
1 cup	sugar
3	eggs, beaten
1½ teaspoons	vanilla
¼ teaspoon	salt
¾ cup	flour
1 cup	chocolate chips
1 cup	chopped pecans

ICING:

¼ cup	butter, softened
2 cups	icing (confectioners') sugar
2 tablespoons	coffee liqueur
	Cinnamon

A great brownie recipe inspired by a fancy specialty coffee! You can use cold coffee in the icing in place of liqueur if you prefer.

1. BROWNIES: Melt butter and chocolate together. Add coffee powder. Stir in sugar, eggs, vanilla and salt, mix well. Add flour and stir to combine. Stir in chocolate chips and nuts. Pour into a greased 9 inch square pan. Bake at 325° F. for about 40 minutes. Cool completely before icing.

2. ICING: In a small bowl beat the butter until light and fluffy. Gradually beat in icing sugar, and continue beating until smooth. Beat in liqueur to combine. Spread icing over the cooled brownies. Sprinkle cinnamon over top. Cut into squares. Store in the refrigerator.

Peanut Butter Brownies

BROWNIES:

⅓ cup	butter
2 squares	(1 oz. each) unsweetened chocolate
⅔ cup	flour
½ teaspoon	baking powder
¼ teaspoon	salt
2	eggs
1 cup	sugar
1 teaspoon	vanilla

TOPPING:

⅓ cup	peanut butter
2 tablespoons	butter, softened
2 tablespoons	sugar
1 tablespoon	flour
1	egg

Always very popular - the chocolate and peanut butter combination makes a very tasty brownie.

1. BROWNIES: Melt butter and chocolate together. Set aside to cool.

2. In a small bowl mix flour, baking powder and salt together.

3. In a large mixing bowl, beat the eggs and sugar together until light. Add the vanilla. Stir in the flour mixture, and the cooled chocolate mixture. Pour into a greased 8 inch square pan.

4. TOPPING: Beat all ingredients together until smooth. Drop spoonfuls of peanut butter mixture over the brownie layer. Run a knife through the cake to marble. Bake at 350° F. for 25 to 30 minutes. Cool, and cut in squares.

German Chocolate Brownies

BROWNIES:

⅓ cup	butter
3 squares	(1 oz. each) unsweetened chocolate
⅔ cup	flour
½ teaspoon	baking powder
¼ teaspoon	salt
2	eggs
¾ cup	white sugar
1 teaspoon	vanilla

TOPPING:

⅓ cup	butter, softened
⅓ cup	brown sugar
¼ cup	light cream
1 cup	flaked coconut

Try this great German chocolate cake topping on top of a rich brownie base.

1. BROWNIES: Melt butter and chocolate together. Set aside to cool.

2. In a small bowl, combine flour, baking powder and salt. In a large bowl beat eggs. Blend in sugar. Add chocolate mixture and vanilla. Stir in flour mixture. Pour into a greased 8 inch square pan. Bake at 325° F. for 15 to 18 minutes. Cool.

3. TOPPING: Cream butter and sugar together. Stir in cream and coconut. Spread over the cooled cake. Preheat broiler. Place brownies under broiler for 1 to 2 minutes, until topping is bubbly. Cool and cut into squares.

Chilled Squares

Nanaimo Bars

BASE:

½ cup	butter
¼ cup	sugar
5 tablespoons	cocoa
1	egg, slightly beaten
1 teaspoon	vanilla
2 cups	graham wafer crumbs
1 cup	coconut
½ cup	chopped walnuts

VANILLA FILLING:

¼ cup	butter
¼ cup	milk
2 tablespoons	custard powder
2 cups	icing (confectioners') sugar
1 teaspoon	vanilla

TOPPING:

4 squares	(1 oz. each) semi-sweet chocolate
1 tablespoon	butter

A Canadian classic. Custard powder can be found in the baking section of the grocery store, or substitute with instant vanilla pudding powder.

1. BASE: Combine butter, sugar, cocoa and egg in a saucepan. Place over simmering water in a double boiler, or over low direct heat. Cook and stir until thick and smooth, about 5 minutes. Remove from heat and stir in vanilla. Add graham wafer crumbs, coconut and nuts and stir to combine. Spread in a greased 9 inch square pan and pack down firmly.

2. VANILLA FILLING: Cream butter. Combine milk and custard powder and blend until smooth. Stir into the butter. Add icing sugar and blend on low speed with mixer until smooth. Stir in vanilla. Spread filling over chocolate layer. Chill for 15 minutes.

3. TOPPING: Melt chocolate and butter together. Spread over the filling. Refrigerate. Cut into bars.

O Henry Bars

1 cup	brown sugar
½ cup	butter
½ cup	milk
1½ cups	graham wafer crumbs
1 cup	chopped walnuts
1 cup	coconut
	Whole graham wafers
	Chocolate icing

We used to have these when we were kids - they are very tasty.

1. Combine brown sugar, butter and milk in a saucepan. Bring to a boil and boil for 1 minute. Remove from heat. Stir in graham wafer crumbs, walnuts and coconut. Line the bottom of an 8 or 9 inch square pan with whole graham wafers. Spread graham wafer crumb mixture over top. Top with another layer of whole graham wafers. Ice with chocolate icing. Refrigerate. Cut into bars.

Lemon Squares

1 can	sweetened condensed milk
½ cup	lemon juice
	Whole graham wafers
	Butter icing

You can't get much easier than this - and yet they turn out to be a fancy and delicious little square - no one would ever guess!

1. Add lemon juice to sweetened condensed milk. Stir until it thickens. Line the bottom of an 8 inch square cake pan with a single layer of graham wafers. Carefully pour the lemon mixture over wafer layer and spread evenly. Top with another layer of graham wafers. Refrigerate 12 hours or overnight. Ice with butter icing. Cut into squares.

Snowdrift Bars

BASE:

½ cup	butter
2	eggs, beaten
1 cup	sugar
½ cup	coconut
1 teaspoon	vanilla
2 cups	graham wafer crumbs
½ cup	chopped walnuts
1½ cups	miniature marshmallows

LEMON BUTTER ICING:

¼ cup	butter, softened
2 cups	icing (confectioners') sugar
2 tablespoons	lemon juice
	Cream

This is a cool and refreshing square recipe - very nice on a hot summer day, great to take along on a picnic.

1. BASE: Melt butter in a saucepan. Add eggs, sugar and coconut. Cook over low heat until thickened, about 10 minutes. Remove from heat and stir in vanilla. Add graham wafer crumbs and walnuts and stir to combine. Fold in miniature marshmallows. Spread in a 9 inch square pan. Chill until firm. Ice with Lemon Butter Icing.

2. LEMON BUTTER ICING: Beat butter until fluffy. Blend in icing sugar and lemon juice. Add enough cream to make a spreadable frosting. Spread frosting on cooled base. Refrigerate. Cut into squares.

Chocolate Rice Krispie Squares

¼ cup	cocoa
3 tablespoons	butter
¼ cup	corn syrup
¼ cup	sugar
3 cups	Rice Krispies cereal

I used to make these as often as I could when I was a kid!

1. Combine cocoa, butter, corn syrup and sugar in a saucepan. Cook and stir over low heat just until the mixture comes to a boil, then remove from heat. Stir in Rice Krispies. Pack into a greased 8 inch square cake pan. Cool and cut in squares.

Cereal Slice

BASE:
½ cup	brown sugar
½ cup	corn syrup
2 cups	Corn Flakes cereal
1 cup	Rice Krispies cereal

ICING:
2 tablespoons	soft butter
1 tablespoon	peanut butter
1 cup	icing (confectioners') sugar
1 teaspoon	vanilla
3 tablespoons	cream

A tasty, crunchy bar, with just a hint of peanut taste in the icing.

1. BASE: Combine brown sugar and corn syrup. Heat over low heat on stovetop, or in the microwave, until the sugar is melted. Do not cook. Remove from heat and stir in Corn Flakes and Rice Krispies. Press into an 8 inch square pan.

2. ICING: Cream butter and peanut butter. Blend in icing sugar and vanilla. Gradually add cream, stirring after each addition. Add enough cream to make a speadable icing, you may need a little more or less. Beat until smooth. Spread icing on cooled base. Refrigerate. Cut into squares.

Mars Bar Rice Krispie Squares

3	Mars bars
¼ cup	butter
2 cups	miniature marshmallows
4 cups	Rice Krispies cereal

An extra special Rice Krispie square!

1. Cut up Mars bars. Combine in a saucepan with butter and marshmallows. Cook and stir over low heat until melted. You can also melt them in the microwave. Remove from heat and stir in Rice Krispies. Pack into a greased 9 inch square cake pan. Cool and cut in squares.

Peanut Butter Squares

BASE:
½ cup	brown sugar
½ cup	corn syrup
1 cup	peanut butter
1 teaspoon	vanilla
1 cup	Corn Flakes cereal
2 cups	Rice Krispies cereal

CARAMEL FROSTING:
¼ cup	butter
½ cup	brown sugar
2 tablespoons	milk or cream
1 cup	icing (confectioners') sugar
1 teaspoon	vanilla

This is Auntie Bess's recipe for a very rich and tasty square.

1. BASE: Combine brown sugar and corn syrup. Heat over low heat on stovetop, or in the microwave, until the sugar is melted. Remove from heat and stir in peanut butter and vanilla. Fold in Corn Flakes and Rice Krispies. Press into an 8 inch square pan.

2. CARAMEL FROSTING: Melt butter. Add brown sugar and stir over low heat for 2 minutes. Add milk and cook and stir until it comes to a boil. Remove from heat and add icing sugar. Beat until creamy. Stir in vanilla. Spread icing on top of the base. Cut into squares. Refrigerate.

Candy

Caramel Corn

2 cups	brown sugar
1 cup	butter
½ cup	corn syrup
¼ teaspoon	cream of tartar
½ teaspoon	baking soda
16 cups	popped popcorn
	Nuts as desired

Easy and fun to make. Pack in fancy tins to give as a nice gift. You can use whatever nuts you like (or none if you don't like nuts). To make it Hawaiian style add pineapple chunks (well drained) with the nuts.

1. Mix brown sugar, butter and corn syrup together in a saucepan. Heat to boiling and boil for 5 minutes. Remove from heat and add cream of tartar and baking soda. It will foam up.

2. Put the popcorn and nuts on a cookie sheet. Pour the sugar mixture over. Bake at 300° F. for about 20 minutes, stirring once. Remove from the oven, cool, and break apart.

Marshmallows

2 packages	plain gelatin
½ cup	cold water
2 cups	sugar
¾ cup	boiling water
½ teaspoon	salt
½ teaspoon	vanilla
	Coconut

The bake shop back home used to make this tasty confection - the squares were rolled in toasted flaked coconut. You can do the same.

1. Add gelatin to cold water. Set aside.

2. Combine sugar and boiling water in a saucepan. Bring to a medium boil and boil for 10 minutes. Remove from heat.

3. Add gelatin mixture to sugar mixture, and beat until stiff. Stir in salt and vanilla. Put in a buttered dish. Cut with a wet knife. Sprinkle with coconut.

Velvet Fudge

3 cups	sugar
2 tablespoons	corn syrup
3 squares	(1 oz. each) unsweetened chocolate
⅛ teaspoon	salt
1 cup	evaporated milk
3 tablespoons	butter
1 teaspoon	vanilla
1 cup	chopped nuts (optional)

We always made fudge around Christmas time. This is my favourite chocolate fudge recipe, from our neighbour back home, Emerald Grierson.

1. In a large saucepan mix sugar, corn syrup, chocolate, salt, evaporated milk and butter. Bring to a boil over medium heat. Cook, stirring constantly until soft ball stage is reached - 236° F. on a candy thermometer. (Or drop a teaspoonful into a cup of cold water - if it forms a soft ball then it is ready, if it spatters apart it is not.) Let cool slightly, and stir in vanilla and nuts if desired. Beat until thick and creamy. Turn into a buttered pan (8 inch square or round pan) and cut into squares.

Brown Sugar Fudge

2 cups	brown sugar
¼ teaspoon	salt
2 tablespoons	corn syrup
2 tablespoons	butter
¾ cup	evaporated milk
1 teaspoon	vanilla
⅔ cup	chopped nuts (optional)

Another favourite - a rich creamy treat.

1. Mix sugar, salt, syrup, butter and evaporated milk together in a large saucepan. Cook over medium heat, stirring constantly, until the soft ball stage is reached (236° F. on a candy thermometer). Remove from heat and let cool. Stir in vanilla and nuts if using. Beat until thick and creamy. Turn into buttered pan (7 inch square or 8 inch round) and cut into squares.

Extra Recipes

Recipe Index

Appetizers 28
- Baked Cranberry Brie 30
- Cheddar Shortbread 30
- Cheese Ball 28
- Guacamole 31
- Hot Crab Dip 28
- Nuts and Bolts 32
- Shrimp Spread 29
- Smoked Salmon Pate 30
- Spinach Dip 32
- Stuffed Mushrooms 29
- Sweet and Sour Meatballs 31

Baked Desserts 128
- Apple Brown Betty 137
- Bread Pudding 139
- Caramel Dumplings 129
- Carrot Pudding 141
- Chocolate Upside Down Cake 133
- Creamy Top of Stove Rice Pudding 138
- Gingerbread With Lemon Sauce 132
- Honey Apple Crisp 139
- Lemon Pudding Cake 129
- Peach Raspberry Cobbler 131
- Pineapple Upside Down Cake 140
- Rhubarb Crunch 136
- Rhubarb Platz 128
- Rhubarb Strawberry Cobbler 135
- Rhubarb Upside Down Cake 130
- Upside Down Chocolate Pudding 134

Baked Squares 157
- Almond Roca Squares 164
- Cherry Slice 168
- Chocolate Chews 161
- Chocolate Pecan Squares 167
- Dream Bars 157
- Granola Bars 164
- Hello Dollies 166
- Honey Date Bars 160
- Jam Squares 161
- Maple Walnut Squares 163
- Matrimonial Cake 158
- Oh Henry Bars 166
- Peanut Butter Bars 160
- Pumpkin Squares 159
- Raspberry Dream Bars 162
- Rocky Road Bars 165

Beef 34
- Beef and Broccoli Stir Fry 42
- Beef and Noodle Casserole 44
- Beef Bourguignon 37
- Braised Garlic Short Ribs 36
- Burgundy Beef Stew 41
- Dad's Deluxe Meat Loaf 44
- Devilled Swiss Steak 39
- Ground Beef Casserole 46
- Ground Beef Porcupines 45
- Hamburger Soup 43
- Homesteader Beef Pie 47
- Mock Duck (Stuffed Steak) 40
- Oven Pot Roast 34
- Shepherd's Pie 43
- Spicy Beef Goulash 38
- Steak and Mushroom Casserole 39
- Steak and Onion Stir Fry 42
- Steak Chili 35
- Sweet and Sour Meatballs 45
- Swiss Steak 36
- Tourtiere 46

Breads 91
- Buttermilk Biscuits 92
- Old Fashioned Bread Stuffing 91
- Yorkshire Pudding 91

Breakfast Dishes 23
- Baked Apple French Toast 25
- Baked Denver Omelet 23
- Breakfast Strata 24
- Pancakes 23

Brownies 169
- Basic Brownies 170
- Blonde Brownies 171
- Chocolate Cheesecake Brownies 169
- German Chocolate Brownies 174

Mochachino Brownies   172
Peanut Butter Brownies   173
Triple Chocolate Brownies   170

Cakes   94
Apple Coffee Cake   103
Banana Cream Cake   99
Buttermilk Chocolate Cake   104
Carrot Cake   94
Chocolate Caramel Pecan Cake   105
Cocoa Cake   97
Graham Wafer Cake   107
Hot Milk Cake   102
Lazy Daisy Oatmeal Cake   101
Mabel's Date Cake   95
Pat's Boiled Raisin Cake   100
Sour Cream Cake   98
The Best Chocolate Cake   96
Yule Log   106

Candy   180
Brown Sugar Fudge   181
Caramel Corn   180
Marshmallows   180
Velvet Fudge   181

Cheesecakes   114
Apple Cheesecake   116
Baileys Marble Cheesecake   117
Chocolate Cheesecake   122
Chocolate Chip Cheesecake   120
Chocolate Turtle Cheesecake   119
Creamy Baked Cheesecake   121
Marble Chocolate Cheesecake   114
Peanut Butter Chocolate Cheesecake   118
Pumpkin Cheesecake   127
Raspberry White Chocolate Cheesecake   125
S'mores Cheesecake   123
Unbaked Cherry Cheesecake   115
Unbaked Chocolate Cheesecake   126
White Chocolate Cheesecake   124

Chilled Desserts   142
Aloha Pineapple Squares   144
Cherry Cha-Cha Pudding   143
Crispy Crunch Torte   143
Khalua Mousse Torte   142
Lemon Dessert Cake   144
Oreo Ice Cream Pie   142
Strawberry Dessert   145

Chilled Squares   175
Cereal Slice   178
Chocolate Rice Krispie Squares   177
Lemon Squares   176
Mars Bar Rice Krispie Squares   178
Nanaimo Bars   175
O Henry Bars   176
Peanut Butter Squares   179
Snowdrift Bars   177

Coffee Cakes   16
Apple Walnut Coffee Cake   20
Cherry Coffee Cake   18
Coffee Cake   19
Coffee Coffee Cake   17
Cranberry Streusel Coffee Cake   16
Rhubarb Streusel Coffee Cake   21
Strawberry Rhubarb Coffee Cake   22

Cookies   148
Boston Cookies   150
Butter Balls   155
Cherry Flips   154
Chocolate Chip Cookies   149
Chocolate Chunk Shortbread   153
Chocolate Shortbread   151
Date Balls   156
Grandma's Shortbread Cookies   151
Irish Cream Balls   154
Java Jems   156
Mocha Disks   152
Molasses Cookies   150
Oatmeal Raisin Cookies   148
Peanut Butter Cookies   149
Pecan Puffs   153
Quick Coconut Oatmeal Cookies   148
Thimble Cookies   152
Unbaked Chocolate Cookies   155

Muffins   8
Banana Muffins   9
Bessie's Bran Muffins   10

Blueberry Muffins   11
Date and Orange Muffins   8
Double Chocolate Muffins   11
Maple Walnut Muffins   14
Morning Glory Muffins   13
Peanut Butter Muffins   10
Rhubarb Pecan Muffins   8
Spiced Apple Muffins   12
Sugar and Spice Muffins   15

Pasta   63
Baked Pasta   69
Baked Rigatoni and Meatballs   72
Beef and Cheese Pasta   63
Beef and Sausage Sauce   75
Beefy Macaroni and Cheese   68
Bolognese Sauce   76
Creamy Baked Pasta   70
Lasagna   64
Macaroni and Cheese   65
Macaroni with Salmon   65
Party Pasta   67
Pasta Florentine   71
Rigatoni With Chili Sauce   77
Rigatoni With Sausage Sauce   74
Spaghetti and Meatballs   73
Spinach Manicotti   66
Tomato Sauce   74
Tuna Florentine   68

Pies   108
Apple Crisp Pie   109
Apple Pie   108
Flapper Pie   113
Never-Fail Pastry   108
Pumpkin Pie   110
Rhubarb Crumble Pie   112
Rhubarb Strawberry Pie   110
Sour Cream Rhubarb Crumb Pie   111

Pork   48
Baked Pork Chops and Apples   51
Barbecued Pork Pot Roast   50
Barbecue Pork Chops   52
Italian Pork Chops   51
Pineapple Pork   49
Pork and Sweet Potato Stew   52

Pork and Yam Bake   49
Pork Chop Casserole   50
Spanish Style Chops   48
Swiss Pork Chops and Vegetables   48

Poultry   53
Chicken Cacciatore   53
Chicken Delight   54
Chicken Dijon Stew   60
Chicken Parmesan   55
Chicken Schnitzel   56
Chicken With Spanish Rice   58
Chicken with Sweet Potato Dressing   59
Crispy Sour Cream Chicken   57
Island Style Chicken   54
Leftover Turkey Casserole   60
Microwave Chicken and Dressing   53

Salads   80
3 Bean Salad   85
Cauliflower Salad   82
Chicken Salad   82
Corn Salad   83
Dilled Salmon Pasta Salad   86
Grandma's Salad Dressing   84
Italian Pasta Salad   85
Mandarin Almond Salad   80
Marinated Coleslaw   81
Mashed Potato Salad   84
Pineapple Carrot Jellied Salad   86
Pineapple Chicken Salad   83
Spicy Coleslaw   81
Waldorf Salad   80

Seafood   61
Salmon Loaf   62
Shrimp Creole Casserole   61

Vegetables   87
Apple Rutabaga Casserole   87
Baked Beans   87
Creamy Mashed Potatoes   89
Garlic Mashed Potatoes   88
Oven Roasted Potatoes   89
Scalloped Potatoes   90
Scalloped Potatoes with Cheese   90
Sweet Potato Casserole   88

Joan Donogh

Joan Donogh launched the Now....you're cooking! website in 1998 to preserve her family's heritage recipes. Today the site receives over 20,000 visitors per month. Many visitors write with their thanks for having found that special recipe "just like Mom used to make." In 2007, Joan launched a new recipe website - Recipes Old and New - encouraging visitors to particpate by sharing their favourite recipes, and rating and reviewing recipes.

Visit www.RecipesOldandNew.com